JIM HAKE

Jim Hake is the Founder and Chairman of Spirit of America, a nonprofit charity that fulfills requests from Americans serving abroad for goods that will help local people. At the request of American troops, Spirit of America has provided millions in assistance to the people of Afghanistan, Iraq and Africa – everything from sandals and school supplies, to sewing machines, irrigation equipment and farming tools. Spirit of America's work improves relations, saves lives, and helps people in need.

The Wall Street Journal calls Jim and the U.S. Marines "a coalition of the can do," and notes, "Jim Hake's organizational insight is to deploy the best practices of the modern U.S. economy" in support of American troops and their humanitarian initiatives.

Jim has been a pioneer in two emerging areas in philanthropy with Spirit of America: direct giving and transparency. Spirit of America donors can direct funds to specific needs and projects, knowing that 100% of their contribution is used for the designated purpose. And, Spirit of America publishes detailed financial statements on its web site quarterly.

Before Spirit of America, Jim was a technology and media entrepreneur and investor. He was a founder of Access Media, one of the very first Internet media companies, and was twice recognized by the World Economic Forum as a Technology Pioneer. His work to advance the Internet was praised by Vice President Al Gore and Speaker Newt Gingrich.

Jim is a graduate of Dartmouth College and the Stanford University Graduate School of Business. He lives in Los Angeles, California, and can be reached at jhake@spiritofamerica.net.

101 Ways to
HELP THE CAUSE
in AFGHANISTAN

101 WAYS TO

HELP THE CAUSE

IN AFGHANISTAN

JIM HAKE

Founder, Spirit of America

SPIRIT of AMERICA

LOS ANGELES, CALIFORNIA

 SPIRIT *of*AMERICA

Spirit of America Press
12021 Wilshire Boulevard, #507
Los Angeles, CA 90025
310-230-5476 Fax: 310-862-4542
staff@spiritofamerica.net

Disclaimer
This publication is designed to educate and provide general information regarding the subject matter covered. The reader is encouraged to review the featured organizations and their work before making any donation or contribution. While the author has taken reasonable precautions in the preparation of this book and believes the facts presented within the book are accurate, neither the publisher nor the author assume any responsibility for errors or omissions. The author and publisher specifically disclaim any liability resulting from the use or application of the information contained in this book.

Publisher's Cataloging-In-Publication information available upon request.

ISBN-13: 978-1-61658-527-3

Printed in the United States of America.
Cover and book design: Patricia Bacall

To the true spirit of America – the initiative, optimism
and generosity of the American people.

CONTENTS

HELP THOSE WHO SERVE

GET INVOLVED

INTRODUCTION

I wrote this book because of two things I've learned in our work at Spirit of America: Americans want to help; and, your help can make a crucial difference in Afghanistan.

There is natural skepticism when someone says, "you can make a crucial difference." Please take a few minutes to read why this is true and how you can use *Help the Cause* to do it.

Here are three examples of how seemingly small things, when done at the right time and place, have a great impact:

The first involves Sergeant First Class (SFC) Jay Smith and US Special Forces in Orgun-e, Afghanistan, a small village near the Pakistani border. Outside their official duties and with donations from Americans back home, Jay and his team did many small but meaningful things to help the villagers. They provided pens, notebooks and school supplies for children, as well as clothing and blankets for families. They started a Little League with boys and girls playing baseball games just for fun. The key to these "small things" was they went directly to the heart of a community and, unlike large aid projects, they were done quickly and produced immediate results.

Jay told me that the things his team did to build relations with the villagers of Orgun-e "saved lives." I thought he was exaggerating. Jay then explained that Al Qaeda had been coming across the border at night and firing rockets on his Special Forces team. Because of the relations Jay and his team built with the villagers, the villagers formed a night watch patrol to protect the Americans. It did indeed save lives.

This is the kind of thing that happens below the radar and that we rarely hear about. It's both extraordinary and extraordinarily simple. When people help people it works.

The second example involves Gunnery Sergeant Shawn Delgado and the Marines in Anbar Province, Iraq. When I met Shawn in Ramadi, Iraq he asked if Spirit of America could provide sandals so children could play outside on streets that were otherwise too hot. In two weeks we provided the sandals he needed.

Shawn told me, "The biggest benefit that Spirit of America provides to the Marine on the 'front line' is that it allows us to approach the populace of an area from another direction. When we come in to potentially help them with some sort of shortfall, we are filling a need that otherwise would not be addressed. Because of all of the negative reports, it is easy to forget that the vast majority of the people are not hostile to us. Spirit of America allows us the tools to be able to approach them on a personal level and to connect with them outside of a hostile encounter."

"Although they were initially skeptical when we arrived, with the gift of shoes and sandals for the kids things changed. The leadership of the village came out and actively engaged us in productive conversations as to how we could provide assistance to them and what they needed to improve their basic quality of life issues. This small gift to the kids helped in opening up lines of communication with the tribal leadership for positive future operations in the area."

Shawn's point is simple but profound. A small thing like a pair of sandals reduces hostility. And, reducing hostility saves lives. It helped open communication and create space where positive relations could develop.

The third example involves 1st Lieutenant Mike Kuiper, serving in Nawa, Afghanistan with the 1st Battalion, 5th Marines (the "1/5"). Nawa is in Helmand Province where there was fierce fighting in the summer of 2009 and where fighting continues in many areas.

Spirit of America received a request from Mike. He asked for solar-powered radios, supplies for local Afghan police, school supplies, Polaroid cameras and instant film, toys and puzzles for children, soccer balls and nets, volleyballs and nets. All these items were intended to help, and build better relations with, the people of Nawa.

Mike said, "Support such as with Spirit of America is vital in convincing the people that we are not enemies of Afghanistan, but friends. This is the way we will win. They'll remember this interaction the rest of their lives, that the Americans loved us and taught us and tried to make this country better."

Of course, our support makes a difference when is it added to the extraordinary commitment and service of our troops and the on-the-ground personnel of the organizations in this book.

General Jim Mattis recently visited the Marines in Nawa. He wrote, "I visited the 1/5 today. The Marines are living in very austere conditions (washing themselves and their clothes in canals, sleeping on the ground, etc). They have thrown the enemy completely off balance, and we walked without helmets/ flak jackets among people who until recently lived in Taliban-dominated areas. Thanks very much for the support you're giving our lads."

The 1/5 Marines are now viewed as a model in Afghanistan: protecting the local population, building positive relations and making progress.

Getting assistance down to the local level works. The examples above involve American troops we know through Spirit of America. But every organization featured in this book has similar stories of how, with the support of Americans back home, a person, a family or a village in Afghanistan was helped by the work they do.

The key is to provide support at the local, even personal, level. The help has to be focused on specific local needs, which requires flexibility, and it has to be fast. This requires a decentralized, grass-roots approach. No one organization can do it alone. That is why this book features the work of 65 different organizations.

Being fast, flexible and decentralized is not the strength of large bureaucracies. But it is a perfect match for Americans who want to help. You don't have to deal with lengthy approval processes. You can set down this book and contribute to a project you find worthy right now.

In *Help the Cause* you'll learn 101 different ways to make a difference at the local level and on the front lines. You'll see how you can reach around the world and have a direct impact on the Afghan people and on the safety and success of our troops.

Each way to help is also a story: about the hopes and struggles of the Afghan people; about the initiative, creativity and courage of the organizations working to help the Afghan people and support our troops; and about the extraordinary work and sacrifice of Americans serving in Afghanistan.

Help the Cause is about people, not politics. We have nearly 100,000 men and women serving in Afghanistan. If you don't support US policy but you do support the troops, *Help the Cause* gives you 101 ways to support them that have nothing to do with politics. You can use this book to help our troops come home sooner, safer and successfully.

Please choose at least one way to help and do it. One small act can change, or save, a life.

I hope *Help the Cause* becomes a larger conversation. You can start by going to www.helpthecause.com, click on "Tell Your Story" and let us know your experience with helping the cause. And, of course, if you know of a great organization or initiative that we haven't included in the book, please tell us.

HOW TO USE THIS BOOK

Help the Cause features 65 different nonprofit, charitable organizations. Organizations have different policies regarding earmarking of donations. Please visit their web sites for complete up-to-date information.

Help the Cause has three sections:

Help The Afghan People: details actions you can take to help Afghan women, children, farmers and more. Our troops emphasize that when you help the Afghan people you also help those who serve.

Help Those Who Serve: provides ways to help those who are serving in Afghanistan and those who have served. You'll discover new opportunities to support our Soldiers, Sailors, Airmen and Marines.

Get Involved: describes how you, your children and your company can get more personally involved. You'll also find ways to spread the word and get others to help the cause.

HELP THE AFGHAN PEOPLE

HELP THOSE WHO SERVE

GET INVOLVED

#1

Afghan Security Forces Winter Clothing and Boots

SPIRIT OF AMERICA

Summary

You can provide winter clothing and boots requested by American troops for Afghan National Army and Police personnel that will help the Afghans be more effective in providing local security.

Description

A critical goal of the United States, NATO and Afghanistan is to prepare Afghan security forces – Army and Police – to provide security, thus reducing the burden on American troops. The more effective the Afghan forces become, the faster American servicemen and women can return home.

Many American servicemen and women are actively engaged in training and patrolling with their Afghan counterparts. While the training and certain equipment is provided by the government, other more personal items are either not provided or not available in some of Afghanistan's remote areas. Helmand Province is one such remote area.

Marines in Helmand Province have asked for winter clothing, fleece pullovers, caps, and boots to give to the Afghan Army and Police personnel who the Marines are training and with whom they are patrolling. The clothing and boots will make the Afghan forces more effective and productive in the tough winter months.

$12 purchases a fleece pullover.

$2.25 purchases an acrylic cap.

$32 purchases a pair of boots.

How to Help

You can make a donation online, by phone or by check. 100% of your contribution will be used to buy and ship the items requested by Americans serving in Afghanistan for use by Afghan security forces.

If donating by mail, make the check payable to Spirit of America and write "ANSF Clothing" in the check memo area to make sure your donation is properly allocated.

Contact Information

Spirit of America
12021 Wilshire Blvd., Suite 507
Los Angeles, CA 90025
800-819-7875
staff@spiritofamerica.net
Organization: www.spiritofamerica.net
Donate to this project: www.spiritofamerica.net/projects/197

Photo credit: Capt Lance Pugsley, USMC

#2

Aid to Refugee Camps

LAMIA AFGHAN FOUNDATION

Summary

You can help provide humanitarian aid and resources that will empower Afghans to ultimately help themselves. The efforts also support service members in remote locations by fostering good relationships between them and the communities.

Description

The Lamia Afghan Foundation provides aid to refugee camps and remote villages in Afghanistan with donations of winter relief items, including: coats, sweaters, boots and socks, shoes, hats, gloves, scarves, sleeping bags, blankets, warm bedding, nutritional support, hygiene products, medical supplies, school supplies and teaching supplies.

The Lamia Afghan Foundation, in conjunction with its partner Afghan Education for A Better Tomorrow, helped provide military tents, flooring and mattresses to four schools (two boys and two girls) in two refugee camps in Afghanistan.

In less than one year, The Lamia Afghan Foundation has airlifted through The Denton Program USAID more than 140,000 pounds of humanitarian aid with another 300,000 pounds of winter relief aid waiting for airlift.

The first 70,000 pounds of aid was distributed during the summer of 2009 by Special Operation Teams stationed at Bagram Air Field, Afghanistan to villages and refugees in remote areas. The remaining 70,000 pounds was distributed in the fall of 2009 by Lamia Afghan Foundation partner Lt. Gen. Zahir Aghbar, President of the Afghan National Olympic Committee in Kabul, Afghanistan, to the neediest in villages and refugee camps.

The mission of The Lamia Afghan Foundation is two-fold. They are dedicated to helping the disadvantaged people of Afghanistan, particularly women and children, by providing humanitarian aid and resources that will empower Afghans through education, skills training and jobs. The organization also seeks to support service members working in remote locations in Afghanistan at Forward Operating Bases.

The formation of The Lamia Afghan Foundation was inspired by a little girl in a red headscarf whose sandaled feet were freezing in the winter of 2007. She begged Lt. Gen. John A. Bradley, the organization's founder, for a pair of boots like he was wearing. Their first meeting was captured in the photo above.

Beautiful LAMIA became the inspiration for the name of the foundation and for the desire to help all the children she represents in this war-torn country who are the real victims of war.

How to Help

You can make a monetary donation online.

You can donate school supplies, medical supplies, nutritional and hygiene items, warm clothing and blankets, and building supplies. Visit the LAF website and read the Giving Guidelines for specific directions.

Contact Information

The Lamia Afghan Foundation
c/o Lt. Gen. and Mrs. John A. Bradley
4014 Skyline Dr
Nashville, TN. 37215
615-783-2899
txmilmom@aol.com
Website: www.lamia-afghanfoundation.org
Donations: www.lamia-afghanfoundation.org/donations.html

Photo credit: Lamia Afghan Foundation

#3

Auto Shop Vocational Training

AFGHAN RELIEF ORGANIZATION

Summary

You can help Afghans receive vocational training for automotive repair, providing them employable skills.

Description

Afghan Relief Organization (ARO) proudly opened the doors of the Technology Education Center (TEC) in Kabul, Afghanistan, in April 2003, during the Spring 2003 Relief Trip. The TEC is located in the Kabul University neighborhood, and has already begun classes in English, vocational and job-skill training. Classes are available for young students and adults, and ARO hopes to initiate "teach the teacher" training to create a network of technology proficient educators, who in turn will educate others.

A mechanical shop area was created at ARO to provide classes in engine diagnostics and repair, auto body repair, and painting.

The course takes fourteen months to complete. In the first three months of the program, trainees receive hands-on instruction in welding and metal works as preparation for the mechanical tasks. Students can then design and fabricate metal parts necessary to their work. The current program can accommodate 30 students.

The purpose of the vocational program in auto mechanics is to provide professional and vocational skills to help students become self sufficient and generate a livable income. Auto mechanic graduates are obtaining jobs with governmental offices, NGOs, embassies and other organizations. Since new vehicles are not readily available, the skills to provide maintenance and repair of automobiles is in high demand.

The auto mechanic course is free to students, a unique feature in Afghanistan. ARO provides educational programs at no cost to students in order to aid low-income families.

The opening reception was held at the ARO TEC in 2005, with guests from government offices, embassies, and organizations aiding the recovery of Afghanistan. Guests cut the ribbon above a tray of "sweets," a tradition to bring luck and happiness.

The TEC is located in a large two-story building, donated for ARO's use, and renovations were completed during the Spring 2003 Relief Trip. The TEC is an approximately 4000 square-foot multi-building structure with an interior courtyard, and can house four large classrooms for computer training, English classes, vocational training and a library area for a variety of resource books and materials. A large conference/lecture room was also built, and is already in use. Guesthouse accommodations are available nearby for visiting educators, and ARO welcomes those who wish to visit and offer their teaching skills.

How to Help

You can make a donation online or by mail.

Contact Information

Afghanistan Relief Organization
P.O. Box 866
Cypress, CA 90630
877-276-2440
Website: www.afghanrelief.org
Donations: www.afghanrelief.org/donate-to-aro

#4

Blankets and Warm Clothing

SPIRIT OF AMERICA

HELP THE AFGHAN PEOPLE

Summary

Provide blankets and warm clothing requested by American servicemen and women to be given to Afghans in need.

Description

American Soldiers and Marines serving in Afghanistan have requested blankets and warm clothing to help Afghans in poverty survive the winter months. These humanitarian goods assist people in need and help our troops improve relations.

Spirit of America has previously provided blankets and warm clothing at the request of Americans serving in Afghanistan. Your support will enable more of this work. Here are three examples.

Spirit of America sent Staff Sgt. Race blankets, boots and socks.

Staff Sergeant Dale Race, US Army, "These people here in this country know that we are here to help and not here to take away any rights, religion or personal freedoms, for they have seen the good we have done."

Spirit of America sent Chaplain Koeman blankets, shoes and winter jackets.

Chaplain Scott Koeman, US Army, "I'm always grieved by the same thing–children living in scandalous conditions. Virtually every day one or more groups from our battalion visit a local village to build relationships with the people. Our Soldiers gain trust and credibility with the local population when they bring humanitarian aid. In turn, this enables us to learn more from the locals how we can stop the enemy that wages war not only against us, but against the stability of the Afghan government. The sooner we can bring stability to this land the sooner the Afghan people prosper and our Forces can return home."

Spirit of America sent blankets to Specialist Llamas.

Specialist Gerardo Llamas, US Army, "I was amazed by their needs and lack of simple things, such as a blanket. Things that we usually take for granted back home. I knew winter here tends to be rough and severe. So I wanted to do something else besides my military duty to help the people of Afghanistan and make a difference in someone's life."

$100 buys 10 winter blankets.

How to Help

You can make a donation online, by phone or by check. 100% of your contribution will be used to purchase and ship requested blankets and clothing.

If donating by check, make check payable to Spirit of America and write "Afghanistan Blankets" in the check memo area to make sure your donation is properly allocated.

If you are a manufacturer and can donate blankets or clothing, please contact Spirit of America directly.

Contact Information

Spirit of America
12021 Wilshire Blvd., Suite 507
Los Angeles, CA 90025
800-819-7875
staff@spiritofamerica.net
Website: www.spiritofamerica.net
Donations: www.spiritofamerica.net/projects/121

Photo credit: SPC Gerardo Llamas, US Army

#5

Build Afghan Schools

AFGHAN CARE TODAY

Summary

You can help build schools to provide Afghan boys and girls with an education, and in the process help to stimulate local Afghan economies.

Description

Afghan Care Today (ACT) believes that terrorism is best fought preemptively through education and opportunity.

By educating the younger generation in traditional subjects, ACT provides parents and their children an alternative to sending their sons to a strictly Islamic fundamentalist program in a madrassa (religious school). Without an alternative or funds to staff a community school, parents have no choice but to send their children to these institutions or simply eliminate their children's education altogether.

Building schools using a local labor force and supplies purchased from local communities stimulates the local economy. This offers Afghans true ownership and control over their own teaching and health care facilities. It also creates a desire to resist outside pressures when confronted by Islamic fundamentalists who want to close down a school that the people of a community have built for their children.

ACT also believes that educational opportunities should be afforded to girls. An education allows these young women to learn new skills, make better choices for the future and empowers them to one day become leaders within their communities.

Costs for the construction and operation of these schools are minimal compared to the United States. The average costs (in USD) are as follows:

One four-room school with an office: $16,000

One teacher's salary for a year: $600

Cost to staff a school for one year: $3200

ACT was launched in late 2008 by former members of the US Army Special Forces Group (A) to provide humanitarian assistance to the people of Afghanistan. They are professionals, with full-time careers ranging from aerospace engineering to medical device sales, who volunteer their time and personal finances in order to help the Afghan people.

How to Help

If you are interested in making a donation, call or email ACT.

Contact Information

Afghan Care Today
3700 State Hwy 35 N
Port Lavaca, Texas 77979
979-229-3193
info@afghancaretoday.com
Website: www.afghancaretoday.org

#6

Bulbs and Supplies for Farmers

SPIRIT OF AMERICA

Summary

You can provide saffron bulbs and supplies to Afghan farmers so they can have a cash crop alternative to poppy.

Description

Sergeant Major James "Mack" McDowell is looking for help to provide Afghan farmers in Zabul Province a cash crop alternative to poppy. In 2007, Mack made a similar request and Spirit of America provided 40,000 saffron bulbs and farm tools. Mack was chosen as a CNN Hero for his efforts. Mack is back in Afghanistan and again seeks support for Afghan farmers. Contributions will buy saffron bulbs, farming tools and other items to benefit the farmers and their families.

Mack says, "The situation here is still not good for the farmers. Some effort has been made to give them good staple crops to grow. Wheat was brought in, in excessive quantities, and given away to many farms. As a result, most farmers in this area grew wheat at the same time, and the market for it crashed. Wheat also takes large amounts of water to grow."

"The locals here use an irrigation system that has been engineered for thousands of years. Underground tunnels called karez feed water along a natural flow line–similar to the Roman Aqueducts. The karez system works, but it is not providing as much water as it used to, because the water table has dropped, partly from over-use like too many wheat crops."

"Every Afghan here talked about getting an alternate crop that used less water. The local Afghans hadn't been talking very long when that word came up again: Zaffron. The farmers know that saffron, or Zaffron as they call it, is grown in Herat where the market for it as an export spice is growing. Saffron also uses a lot less water to grow than wheat or many other staples; all the farmers seem to know that too. The farmers here could use saffron to diversify the crops grown locally, and to lighten the load on the ancient underground Karez system."

"The biggest problem seems to be their need for an alternative crop that is not poppy related, has a high cash value, and does not use more water than the karez system can supply. If Spirit of America could come up with saffron, the farmers here would put it to good use."

$100 buys 400 saffron bulbs.

$60 buys 50 pairs of work gloves.

$10 buys a hoe.

How to Help

You can make a donation online, by phone or by check. 100% of your contribution will be used to buy and ship the items requested.

If donating by check, make payable to Spirit of America and write "Saffron Bulbs" in the check's memo area.

Contact Information

Spirit of America
12021 Wilshire Blvd., Suite 507
Los Angeles, CA 90025
800-819-7875
staff@spiritofamerica.net
Website: www.spiritofamerica.net
Donations: www.spiritofamerica.net/projects/180

Photo credit: James McDowell

#7

Child Care Education

CHILDFUND INTERNATIONAL

Summary

You can provide Afghan children with a safe environment where they can learn and grow by supporting educational programs for their family and community members.

Description

War turns everyone's lives upside down, especially children. Because of this, ChildFund International has worked in Afghanistan since 2001, assisting more than 500,000 children and family members.

ChildFund strives to create environments where children can learn, play and grow. To do this, the children must first feel safe. That's why the organization created Child Well Being Committees, which are designed to involve everyone in the protection of the children in the community. Parents, community members and government staff are trained regarding basic child protection issues, deinstitutionalizing services for orphanages, and family preservation programs.

ChildFund supports community-based literacy classes for rural children and youth. Teachers are trained on classroom procedures that are conducive to children's development and advocate against corporal punishment in the schools. ChildFund helps children regain a sense of normalcy by providing recreational activities, giving special attention to activities for girls.

Health services are also high on the organization's list of priorities for children and their families. ChildFund constructs health posts and provides equipment, medical supplies and training for health workers. There are also programs to connect people in need with assistance through referral services.

In order to help create stable environments, ChildFund helps implement micro-finance programs in post-conflict northern Afghanistan. The loans assist families, many of whom fled to other countries or were living in Internally Displaced People camps, to secure loans and equipment for their ventures.

It only takes one person or one donation to make a difference. Forrest Ewens' family is the perfect example of that.

As a first lieutenant in the US Army, Forrest Ewens had a knack for putting a smile on the children's faces in Afghanistan, often sneaking them treats. But in 2005, at the age of 25, Forrest was killed in the line of duty. His mission to help the Afghan people lives on in the form of a well that brings clean water to 500 families in the remote Samady Village in Badakhshan Province in northeast Afghanistan.

Thanks to Forrest's parents, Michael and Carol Ewens of Gig Harbor, Washington, the well means the community now has clean drinking water and sanitation facilities.

Before the well was built in the village, the children, particularly girls, had to walk to nearby villages to get water. They often waited several hours in long lines to take home only a few gallons of water. If water was not available, the children and their families would have to rely on river water, putting them at high risk for illnesses from water-borne diseases.

How To Help

You can make a donation online or by phone.

Contact Information

ChildFund International
2821 Emerywood Parkway
Richmond, VA 23294
800-776-6767
questions@childfund.org
Website: www.childfund.org
Donations: www.childfund.org/make-a-donation.aspx

Photo credit: ChildFund International

#8

Classrooms Sponsor Afghan Children

WAR KIDS RELIEF

Summary

You can give US students the opportunity to build positive relationships with their Afghan peers by teaching one another about their lives.

Description

War Kids Relief's US/Afghan Junior Investor Program gives US students the opportunity to build positive relationships with their Afghan peers by teaching one another about their lives. This groundbreaking program will also give US students the opportunity to co-invest in the vocational training of their Afghan peers. US students will learn from their Afghan friends as they receive training to develop sustainable, market-based solutions in order to strengthen their local economies and help them avoid recruitment into insurgent groups as a means to an end.

American children have little knowledge of the realities of life for young people in other cultures, especially war-affected areas. Due to the war in Afghanistan, many have an inaccurate understanding of Afghan culture and are unable to put a human face to this country.

Due to decades of war, Afghanistan has become a breeding ground for extremist ideology and children are its most vulnerable citizens. Many young Afghans also have an inaccurate and/or negative image of Americans due to lack of exposure and misinformation.

Step One: Education – Putting a human face on modern Afghan society.

Together with partners in the Cannon Falls, MN, schools and P.E.C.A., a non-profit organization that builds schools in Afghanistan, WKR will create a teaching "package" for American middle/high-school teachers to use in their classrooms.

Step Two: Investment – Creating opportunities for kids to change the world.

After finishing the basic curriculum, the American class does a project to raise $100, which will be used to sponsor one Afghan student's vocational training for one year. Through this entrepreneurial program, each Afghan student will be able to create a small and viable business by graduation. Similar to micro-credit lending, the American students are investing in the success of an Afghan student who they will want to see succeed. Instead of a return on a financial investment, the US students will have the opportunity to learn first hand about how the $100 is being used to effect change, thus, following the ripple effect.

While the Afghan student learns their trade of choice (honey production, brick making, fennel oil production, carpentry or tailoring) and is training to be a businessperson in Afghanistan (studying marketing, pricing, distribution and sales), the sponsoring class in the United States learns at the same time. American teachers and students receive monthly updates from the Afghan student and are able to ask questions of the students. This provides an invaluable, multi-faceted learning experience and cultural exchange.

How to Help

You can donate online through Paypal.

Contact Information

War Kids Relief
P.O. Box 141
Dennison, Minnesota 55018
612-414-7801
dina@warkidsrelief.org
Website: www.warkidsrelief.org
Donations: http://warkidsrelief.org/donate

#9

Computer Education for Children

HELP THE AFGHAN CHILDREN

Summary

You can change the lives of Afghan girls and boys at community-based model schools by supporting HTAC's computer education program.

Description

As the first organization to introduce computer education into Afghan public schools, Help the Afghan Children (HTAC) has been at the forefront of providing computer literacy skills to more than 27,000 Afghan high school students. The computer programs give the students a pathway to become proud, productive citizens of their country.

Each HTAC school has a fully-functional computer lab with computers, a network printer, and projector and screen. Since electricity is scarce in many areas, the schools also have a generator.

Students learn key skills in Microsoft Windows, Word, and Excel. Twelfth grade students are also taught PowerPoint. For the HTAC schools that are equipped, students also learn how to navigate the Internet.

Since the program was introduced in 2003, more than 95% of the enrolled students (97% of which are girls) have become computer literate. Many of the graduating seniors are using their computer skills to gain good jobs in Afghanistan's emerging information technology marketplace.

HELP THE AFGHAN PEOPLE

For boys, having computer skills enables them to avoid joining the ranks of unemployment, a critical problem in many of Afghanistan's cities. Also, boys who find work tend to be far less vulnerable to extremist views and groups. For many girls, having computer skills is an empowering experience, giving them a practical opportunity to escape poverty, early forced marriage and child-bearing.

Twelfth grader Hassina explains why computer education is so important to her and other young women.

"In Afghanistan, a very small percentage of girls have good computer skills and this must change for our country to prosper," said Hassina. "My parents are very happy that I am learning about computers and I want to use these skills when I become a teacher."

How To Help

You can make a donation online or by check.

Contact Information

Help the Afghan Children (HTAC)
3900 Jermantown Road, Suite 300
Fairfax, VA 22030
703-848-0407
Stephen@htac.org
Website: www.htac.org
Donations: http://htac.org

#10

Counseling and Training for Vulnerable Afghans

PHYSIOTHERAPY AND REHABILITATION SERVICES FOR AFGHANISTAN

Summary

You can help the most vulnerable people in Afghanistan receive the training they need to take care of themselves and other Afghans in need.

Description

Physiotherapy and Rehabilitation Services for Afghanistan (PARSA) works with women, orphans, the disabled, and the vulnerable population in Afghanistan. The "hands on" organization specializes in training Afghans to help their own people. By working directly in the orphanages and providing training to Afghans in village and province settings, PARSA is creating healthier communities.

PARSA's team of professionals includes physiotherapists, psychosocial trainers, and social workers who support the organization's economic and education programs by working with people or children with multiple challenges. Afghans get support that is personalized, culturally appropriate, and effective. PARSA's staff works with the severely mentally ill, orphaned children who are experiencing difficulties because of disabilities or war trauma, and widows in need of peer-counseling training. PARSA's employees are mostly Afghans who work with a handful of international workers.

The organization does a tremendous amount of training to enable Afghans to better assist and help their own. One of the programs trains adults to be "Good Mothers" and "Good Fathers" within the orphanages. The adults work directly with orphans and help identify the children with the most dire situations, medically and emotionally. PARSA also trains university-level students to be social workers and help other Afghans struggling with mental health problems and Post Traumatic Stress.

HELP THE AFGHAN PEOPLE

Disabled Afghans are invited to work in the PARSA tailoring shop. There, items are made that can later be sold at bazaars and on international bases, bringing in much-needed funds for the organization to further its work.

An Afghan in the psychosocial training program wrote to express how PARSA has made a difference.

"With my compliments I wanted to share my feelings of my session with you, indeed it went very useful and effective."

"I found the focusing session with you very useful for myself; I noticed many positive changes in myself. As before I had negative thoughts about myself I couldn't interact with friends and family the way I had to; but after the sessions pleasantly with you and learning how to carry it on with myself individually made me strong in facing these negative thoughts and controlling them. Today whenever I think, I can't take decision or I think negatively, with focusing session; I can solve it very easily. I'm very happy; I can interact with friends and family very well."

"I believe focusing is a very comfortable and easy way to get into yourself, listen to yourself, and give time to yourself and meanwhile in taking decisions."

"For me focusing was a very good way to get out of those negativities by accepting them and finding positive thoughts."

"With great honor; thank you."

How To Help

You can make a donation online or by check to the address below. If you would like to donate to a specific program, make a note in the memo.

You can also sign-up for the monthly newsletter to find out about the most current needs and additional ways to help.

Contact Information

PARSA
PO Box 31292
Seattle, WA 98103
United States
+93 799020588
mgustav@mac.com; fieryglass@gmail.com
Website: www.afghanistan-parsa.org
Donations: www.afghanistan-parsa.org/donations

#11

Dental Kits for Afghan Kids

OPERATION GIVE

Summary

You can provide medical supplies and dental hygiene kits to the children of Afghanistan, thereby helping improve relations between service members and the communities.

Description

Operation Give provides toys, educational and medical supplies and other relief to war-torn nations around the world. Supplies are sent to deployed service members who then distribute the items throughout the community. These efforts help service members win the hearts and minds of the people where they are stationed, improving relationships.

Operation Clean Teeth is an Operation Give project that strives to improve the dental hygiene of children. The organization is collecting supplies to create Clean Teeth Kits. The kits contain items such as toothbrushes, toothpaste, dental floss, mouthwash, and individual tissue packs. After the children receive the free kits, they will be taught how to properly take care of their teeth which can improve overall health.

Operation Medical Supplies provides items such as wheelchairs, walkers, crutches, prosthetic arms and legs, hospital equipment, and children's equipment for spinal cord injuries. These supplies help injured children regain some of their freedom and can improve their healing.

Operation Health helps injured and hospitalized children make use of the medical supplies Operation Give donates. The program arranges to send doctors abroad to perform surgeries. The donated prosthetic limbs are both new and used, but each must be custom fitted for the patient. Donations also help purchase retinas so patients who have lost their sight, often the result of an explosion, can receive the surgery they need to see again.

Operation Give supports a variety of efforts that aim to improve the lives of children in war-torn countries. The organization supplies baseball and soccer sports equipment, a variety of toys and stuffed animals, school supplies, and art supplies. It also holds an annual stocking drive, beginning in August, called Operation Christmas Stocking. Operation Give collects pre-filled Christmas stockings and gift boxes that are shipped to service members in Afghanistan and Iraq.

How To Help

You can make a monetary donation online or by mail.

You can gather and ship needed items to the Operation Give warehouse. Visit the Operation Give website to see a complete list of programs and the new or slightly used items needed.

Contact Information

Operation Give
2295 South 900 West
Salt Lake City, Utah 84119
801-259-6336
Donations: www.operationgive.org

Operation Give Warehouse
c/o Mesa Systems
2275 South 900 West
Salt Lake City, Utah 84119
wigglesholton@yahoo.com
Website: www.operationgive.org

#12

Education and Opportunity for Nangarhar Women

SPIRIT OF AMERICA

Summary

Captain C.J. Scott, serving in Nangarhar with the US Army, believes that "the women of Afghanistan are the future of the country, especially in this rural environment." You can help Captain Scott and his combat engineers provide goods to assist women in Nangarhar.

Description

Captain Scott, with the 4th Brigade Special Troops Battalion, and his combat engineers have a "long-term goal...to improve female education and opportunities in a sustainable manner." They are focusing on the female population for "education and economics as they are the forgotten and underappreciated demographic in this complex region."

Captain Scott describes the condition in their area of operation and the specific needs of Afghan women, "We operate in southern Nangarhar, south of Jalalabad. The local villages are primarily agricultural multi-family communes that live along rivers fed by snowmelt from the Tora Boras. Life is hard. The river valleys maintained green vegetation throughout the hot summer, and only seem to dry out in the coldest part of the winter. Most villages are a collection of a few families from the same sub-tribe. The women tend to the gardening and children, while the men work the larger fields and livestock."

"We will distribute the supplies through the local Maliks and tribal elders, with our oversight. We have used a Female Engagement Team (female US Soldiers and a female interpreter) in the past with great success. The idea is to support the local leadership while fostering goodwill with security forces. I am more than a little excited about the support you will be able to provide."

Your donation will purchase the book bags, domestic items and sewing supplies requested by Captain Scott to empower Afghan women.

How to Help

You can make a donation online, by phone or by check. 100% of your contribution will be used to buy and ship the needed goods requested by Captain Scott for women in Nangarhar.

If donating by check, make the check payable to Spirit of America and write "Nangarhar Women" in the check memo area to make sure your donation is properly allocated.

Contact Information

Spirit of America
12021 Wilshire Blvd., Suite 507
Los Angeles, CA 90025
800-819-7875
staff@spiritofamerica.net
Website: www.spiritofamerica.net
Donations: www.spiritofamerica.net/projects/185

Photo Credit: SGT Jennifer Cohen, US Army

#13

Education, Support and Advocacy for Women

FEMINIST MAJORITY FOUNDATION

Summary

You can help advance the rights of women and girls in Afghanistan and support their participation in Afghanistan's future.

Description

The Feminist Majority Foundation has been a tireless advocate for, and supporter of, women and women's rights in Afghanistan since 1997. The Foundation brought together leading human rights and women's organizations to condemn the Taliban's human rights abuses against women and girls and to increase awareness of their suffering. The Foundation was successful in preventing recognition of the Taliban by the United States and United Nations, increasing the admission of Afghan women and girls as refugees and increasing humanitarian aid to Afghanistan.

With its Campaign for Afghan Women and Girls, the Foundation is working to ensure that women are an essential part of the solution for Afghanistan's future. The Campaign is comprised of several elements, each of which offers an opportunity to support Afghan women and protect their rights. The Campaign for Afghan Women and Girls includes:

Action Teams for Afghan Women and Girls. Action Teams are based in the United States. They work to raise public awareness of Afghan women's issues and raise funds to support Afghan-women-led non-governmental organizations (NGOs).

Afghan Women's Scholarship Program. The Foundation provides scholarships as well as supplemental assistance (for books and expenses) that enable Afghan women to pursue study in the United States.

Direct Assistance to Women's Organizations. The Foundation provides funding and technical assistance to nonprofit organizations led by Afghan women.

Afghan Women's Craft Project. The Craft Project sells online crafts made by Afghan women. All proceeds go to benefit Afghan women and girls.

How to Help

You can make a donation to support the Campaign for Afghan Women and Girls online or by check.

You can buy Afghan crafts online. The Foundation sells beautiful pillow covers made by Afghan women.

You can join an Action Team to raise awareness and raise funds. Contact the Feminist Majority Foundation directly.

Contact Information

Feminist Majority Foundation
1600 Wilson Boulevard, Suite 801
Arlington, VA 22209
866-444-3652
Website: www.feminist.org/afghan/index.asp
Donations: www.feminist.org/afghan/index.asp
Buy Afghan Crafts: www.feminist.org/afghan/index.asp

#14

Essential Supplies for Children

OPERATION INTERNATIONAL CHILDREN

Summary

You can provide school supplies, blankets, clothing, and sports equipment that will be sent to the US military in Afghanistan to distribute directly to children.

Description

Operation International Children (OIC) was created to give concerned Americans a way to reach out to war-stricken children by supporting our troops in their efforts to assist them. Working directly with troops, OIC has delivered more than a quarter of a million school supply kits, along with more than half a million toys and thousands of blankets, backpacks, pairs of shoes, Arabic-language books, and sets of sports equipment, all of which have been distributed to children.

Schools in these areas are small, overcrowded, and lack the essential tools the children need to receive a good education. By providing the school supplies, the children are given a little piece of hope. Each school supply kit includes a pair of blunt-end scissors, one ruler with metric markings, 12 new pencils with erasers, a pencil sharpener, large eraser, box of colored pencils, package of notebook paper, composition book, three folders, and a zippered pencil bag.

OIC also provides blankets and shoes, two essential items for children living in areas where heaters are difficult to come by and temperatures often drop to freezing at night. These efforts help our troops foster goodwill in the communities in which they work, and bring brighter futures to children in desperate need.

HELP THE AFGHAN PEOPLE

The idea for the grass-roots program came after actor Gary Sinise (Forrest Gump, Apollo 13, CSI: NY), visited Iraq.

"On my second trip to Iraq in November of 2003, I saw a beautiful interaction between our Soldiers and the Iraqi children," recalls Gary. "The kids were loving our Soldiers and they were so grateful to them for having liberated them from Saddam Hussein. It was a tremendous feeling to see these children hugging and kissing our Soldiers, cheering them with the thumbs up sign and in broken English saying, 'I love you!'"

In early 2004, Gary and author Laura Hillenbrand (Seabiscuit: An American Legend) joined in partnership with People to People International and its President and CEO, Mary Eisenhower, granddaughter of President Dwight D. Eisenhower. Formerly called Operation Iraqi Children, the program has expanded its mission, sending additional school supplies to Afghanistan and other nations, where American troops are distributing them to children in need. OIC plans to continue to broaden its efforts across the world.

How to Help

You can made monetary donations online, or by mailing a check to the donation address below. 100% of these donations go to purchase supplies for children and offset shipping costs.

You can build and send school supply kits yourself, or start a school supply kit drive in your community. Visit OIC online to find kit instructions.

If you are in the Kansas City, MO area, you can volunteer at the OIC warehouse. Call OIC for available days and times.

Contact Information

Monetary Donations: Operation International Children
911 Main Street, Ste: 2110, Kansas City, MO 64105
Supply Donations: OIC Warehouse
1529 Atlantic, North Kansas City, MO 64116
816-241-7321
OICwarehouse@ptpi.org
Website: www.Operationinternationalchildren.org
Donations: www.ptpi.org/donations/Default.aspx

Photo credit: Operation International Children

#15

Farming and Building Tools

SPIRIT OF AMERICA

Summary

You can help Afghans earn a better living and rebuild their communities by providing farming and building tools (wheelbarrows, shovels, picks, rakes).

Description

At the request of American servicemen and women, Spirit of America provides Afghan farmers with tools. The tools improve the farmers' productivity and build better relations.

One new request comes from Marines 4th Civil Affairs Group in Helmand Province, Afghanistan.

Staff Sergeant Anthony Weiss explains the need, "I am with the 4th Civil Affairs Detachment out of DC, currently working in Afghanistan with multiple teams pushed out around Helmand Province. 4th CA DET works hand in hand with the local people to help rebuild of local communities. Some joke we are the hippies of the Marine Corps as we care so much about helping the locals."

"The teams are trying to help the local farmers change their habits for growing poppy. Part of that initiative is to give them better tools that will last longer than a season. The planting season is approaching so I hope that you can help the team get the material to help this transition to a new crop. We are looking for shovels, rakes, scythes, and wheelbarrow. I hope that Spirit of America can help us in our mission to rebuild Afghanistan for the people."

Lt. Colonel Leonard Defrancisci further details how the tools they provide the local Afghans will be used, "The farming tools will be used throughout Helmand

River Valley, specifically in Nawa, Garmsir and Khan Neshin. The farmers grow a wide range of crops, including wheat and corn. A big emphasis is on alternate crops (other than poppy), so any incentive to grow crops other than poppy goes a long way for the Afghans to make the switch."

"We will also use the tools for work programs that will clean district centers and bazaars to make them more suitable for trade and governance, which enhances economic opportunity. We will manage about four cash for works programs creating about 50 jobs each and will restore several shops in the bazaars and make them usable for more shop owners. We will also clean and repair irrigation canals, many of which have experienced significant decay over the years."

$45 buys a wheelbarrow.

$25 buys a farm-grade shovel.

$12 buys 10 pairs of work gloves.

How to Help

You can make a donation online, by phone or by check. 100% of your contribution will be used to buy and ship tools requested by Americans serving in Afghanistan for the Afghan people.

If donating by check, make the check payable to Spirit of America and write "Afghanistan Tools" in the check memo area to make sure your donation is properly allocated.

If your business can donate tools in quantity, please email or call Spirit of America.

Contact Information

Spirit of America
12021 Wilshire Blvd., Suite 507
Los Angeles, CA 90025
800-819-7875
staff@spiritofamerica.net
Website: www.spiritofamerica.net
Donations: www.spiritofamerica.net/projects/184

Photo Credit: SSgt William Greeson, USMC

#16

Firewood and Blankets for Winter Survival

UNITED METHODIST COMMITTEE ON RELIEF

Summary

You can help Afghan families survive the winter by providing them with relief supplies like blankets and firewood.

Description

The United Methodist Committee on Relief (UMCOR) is an organization of the United Methodist Church focusing on humanitarian aid in more than 80 countries. UMCOR has been operating in Afghanistan since 2002 and focuses on aid in the areas of health and education, reconstruction and agricultural development, as well as emergency response.

UMCOR supply kits help care for the most vulnerable people during times of crisis. They sustain everyday life by providing basic necessities to people who lack ready access to essential supplies.

The organization is currently constructing seventy-five shelters in the Khak-e-Jabar District of Kabul Province. In order to complete construction, UMCOR has provided building supplies, while labor has been provided by the beneficiaries of these shelters. The organization also provides winterization materials such as blankets, wood burning stoves and firewood so that families can survive the winter. In January 2009, UMCOR distributed blankets to 3900 families in Afghanistan.

Additionally, UMCOR has helped refugees re-entering Afghanistan to construct permanent homes and rebuild their communities. In the Wardak province of Afghanistan, UMCOR has helped returning refugees to construct homes and support their living through UMCOR's Sustainable Agriculture and Development project.

Twenty-eight year old Mirwais was able construct a permanent home for his family with the support of UMCOR, and received goats from UMCOR's development project.

"UMCOR's help was very good and timely and useful," said Mirwais. "If this organization had not helped me, I would have had to leave my home and return to Pakistan with my family.'"

How to Help

You can donate online, by phone or by check. You can make a specific donation to Afghan projects by donating to Afghanistan Emergency, UMCOR Advance.

You can also donate a relief supply kit or $200 toward the construction of a new home in Afghanistan through the UMCOR Gift Catalog.

You can volunteer your time at relief supply depot. Visit the UMCOR website for more information.

Contact Information

United Methodist Committee on Relief
475 Riverside Drive, Room 330
New York, NY 10115
800-554-8583
umcor@gbgm-umc.org
Website: www.umcor.org
Donations: www.umcor.org

HELP THE AFGHAN PEOPLE

#17

Food and Jobs for Families in Kabul

CARE

Summary

You can provide families in Kabul with jobs that enable them to buy food and other essentials.

Description

In response to the rising food insecurity problem in Afghanistan, particularly in the urban capital of Kabul, CARE implemented a large Cash-for-Work project. Currently, access to food is challenged because of drought and rising food prices. The project is aimed at getting money into the hands of vulnerable Afghans so they are able to survive through this difficult period.

This construction and jobs project will contribute to urban infrastructure by focusing on improving local amenities and services. It has been designed with the support and input of the local authorities including relevant ministries and in particular, the Kabul Municipality.

A total of 50,035 households will be assisted, resulting in a benefit to more than 250,000 people. Special focus is given to women and women-headed households by focusing on activities suitable to the local area.

This project is just one of ten programs CARE conducts in Afghanistan.

CARE's mission is to serve individuals and families in the poorest communities in the world. CARE assists the Afghan people by:

- Strengthening capacity for self-help
- Providing economic opportunity
- Delivering relief in emergencies
- Influencing policy decisions at all levels
- Addressing discrimination in all its forms

CARE places special focus on working alongside poor women because, equipped with the proper resources, women have the power to help whole families and entire communities escape poverty.

How To Help

You can donate online, by phone, or by mail. Reference program AFG048 to help support the Food Insecurity Response for Urban Population of Kabul (FIRUP-K).

Contact Information

CARE
Gift Center
PO Box 1871
Merrifield VA 22116-9753
800-422-7385
info@care.org
Website: www.care.org
Donations: www.care.org/donate

#18

Girls School in Bagram

SPIRIT OF AMERICA

Summary

You can provide school supplies, backpacks, clothing, and personal hygiene items to help schoolgirls who were previously denied an education.

Description

The female literacy rate in Afghanistan is estimated at only 12%. Educating and empowering young women is an important component of change and a better future for the country.

Rachel Hudak, stationed at Bagram Airfield, wants to help the girls at a school near the base.

Rachel writes, "I am often asked what I need or what can be done to help. Well, I finally found something that I am pouring my heart into. This is a project of collecting school supplies, basic hygiene items, and 'girlie' items for the local girls' school here in Afghanistan. It's approximately 10 miles away from our base. Girls are only allowed to attend up to the 8th grade. This is an exceptional opportunity that we can provide some very needed basic necessities to them. It's hard to imagine a country where you cannot go to school because you are a girl. This struck a chord with me."

"The school consists of eight classes, ranging between 150-225 students. Numbers vary since the girls must walk up to an hour to attend classes. Basic school supplies needed for the year are pens, markers, crayons, paper, mechanical pencils, colored pencils, and folders."

"At the beginning of the new school year (February 2010), a backpack and school supplies collection will start. The goal is to distribute more than 225 backpacks.

HELP THE AFGHAN PEOPLE

"Female Soldiers and officers teach basic hygiene to the girls, such as face and hand washing and dental care. Hygiene items needs for the girls are soaps, lotion, hair brushes, hair ties, shampoo, conditioner, toothbrushes, and toothpaste. They also like to provide the young girls with fun items like plastic jewelry, nail polish, and head bands."

"Cold weather items, such as shoes, boots, coats, hats, gloves and scarves are always in high demand."

$2,250 buys all 225 backpacks needed for this project.

$1,125 buys all 225 hygiene kits needed for this project.

$375 buys 25 winter coats.

$100 buys 10 pairs of shoes.

How to Help

You can make a donation online, by phone or by check. 100% of your contribution will be used to buy and ship the items requested for the Bagram Girls School. If more funds are contributed than needed for this school, they will be used to help other schools for girls in Afghanistan.

If donating by check, make the check payable to Spirit of America and write "Bagram Girls School" in the check memo area to make sure your donation is properly allocated.

Contact Information

Spirit of America
12021 Wilshire Blvd., Suite 507
Los Angeles, CA 90025
800-819-7875
staff@spiritofamerica.net
Website: www.spiritofamerica.net
Donations: www.spiritofamerica.net/projects/191

Photo credit: Rachel Hudak

#19

Greenhouse Vocational Training

AFGHAN RELIEF ORGANIZATION

Summary

You can help Afghans learn how to grow and preserve food, while teaching them the benefits of healthy diets full of fresh foods.

Description

The Seeds for Afghanistan project, created in October 2001, partnered with Afghan Relief Organization (ARO) in 2003. Seeds for Afghanistan has collected and distributed more than 800,000 vegetable, herb and flowers seeds to farmers, families, widows, schools, orphan centers and others.

More than five years of drought, combined with two and a half decades of war, have devastated the once abundant home gardens, family farms and flowering pathways of Afghanistan. Hundreds of home gardeners, individuals, nurseries and seed companies have contributed seeds as part of this simple, highly successful grassroots effort. Among the donors are Seeds of Change, Botanical Interests, Inc. and Seed Savers.

ARO constructed a greenhouse, or "gulkhana," at its Technical Education Center (TEC) in Kabul to reintroduce techniques of home gardening to students. The greenhouse offers a unique and practical educational opportunity, teaching students to grow and preserve food, while encouraging a healthy diet of fresh foods. The beauty of the greenhouse also offers a welcome relief to those who have witnessed the ongoing destruction of war.

Future plans of Seeds for Afghanistan include additional greenhouses, and instruction in organic gardening, composting and Permaculture techniques. Small-scale fresh food production can help create sustainable communities.

HELP THE AFGHAN PEOPLE

The Afghan diet is primarily wheat, fruits, nuts and meat. Popular vegetables include tomatoes, corn, zucchini, summer squash, eggplant, garlic, leek, onion, scallion, radish, pumpkin, cucumbers, peppers, chiles, carrots, spinach and lettuce, among others. The primary herbs utilized for food are cilantro, basil, oregano, mint and garlic.

How to Help

You can make a donation online or by mail. Include "Seeds for Afghanistan" on the subject line of your check.

You can donate a variety of seeds to the project. Visit the ARO website for specific guidelines.

Contact Information

Afghanistan Relief Organization
P.O. Box 866
Cypress, CA 90630
877-276-2440
Website: www.afghanrelief.org
Donations: www.afghanrelief.org/donate-to-aro

#20

Homes for Afghan Families

HABITAT FOR HUMANITY

Summary

You can help build homes for Afghan families in need.

Description

At least two-thirds of the Afghans live in sub-standard housing. Half a million homes were destroyed in major cities in the long years of war, according to the United Nations. The scale of destruction in rural areas is not as well documented, but just as intense.

Since the fall of the Taliban government in 2001, there has been an increase in demand for housing. More than 4.5 million refugees have returned from neighboring countries. Others who are displaced within Afghanistan have also returned to their own towns or cities.

The influx has pushed up the prices of land and construction materials. These pressures are particularly acute in urban areas where three-in-four Afghans live in poverty. Lack of clean water is common. Electricity is intermittently available in urban areas and non-existent in most rural areas.

Habitat for Humanity Afghanistan began its program in the northern province of Balkh in 2002. Habitat provided First Shelter homes to meet the demands of families in desperate need of immediate shelter. With no mortgage repayments required for First Shelter homes, costs were kept low by involving families and communities in construction.

First Shelter homes used traditional mud bricks, mud and straw plastering, wooden doors and windows. Each house measured about 36 square meters. The buildings were designed to include two areas where people could live and work, earning a living, by carpet weaving for example, with a traditional domed roof to enhance temperature control.

In November 2004, Habitat started a Save & Build housing microfinance program in Yaka-Toot village near Mazar-i-Sharif, the capital of Balkh province. Under this model, 10 to 12 families form a group to save for the cost of building houses. When they have saved enough for the cost of one house, Habitat and its partners contribute the costs of another two houses and construction begins. The group repeats the savings cycle until all the member families have been housed.

Save & Build was extended to the villages of Ali Abad and Turabi, just east of Mazar-i-Sharif in 2005. The savings groups each comprised an average of 17 families. Construction began in July 2005, and by September 2008, more than 180 houses had been completed.

How To Help

You can donate online, by phone, or by check. For other ways to donate, such as employee matching and gifting, visit the Habitat for Humanity website.

If you represent a corporation willing to donate a large supply of materials, please email gik@habitat.org.

Contact Information

Habitat for Humanity International
121 Habitat Street
Americus, GA 31709-3498
800-422-4828
Website: www.habitat.org
Donations: www.habitat.org

#21

Instant Cameras and Film

SPIRIT OF AMERICA

Summary

You can provide instant cameras and film used by Marines to take snapshots and give them as gifts to Afghan families and children.

Description

This is an opportunity to brighten the day of an Afghan child or family.

The Marines use instant photos as an opportunity for positive interaction with local people in Nawa, Afghanistan. This builds closer, more positive relations and makes the Marines safer and more successful.

1st Lieutenant Mike Kuiper explains, "The Polaroid cameras help start conversations with locals that lead to relationships. I included some pictures in the previous mail to show the successes we are having. Notice how happy the people are to have a picture of themselves or their families. With an average salary of $5.00 a day, most families can't afford a picture of anyone in the family. They love getting pictures of themselves, and have learned to come up and ask for "atkas" or "picture" in Pashto. Taking pictures of kids has helped them not be afraid of us, and shows we are friends. Winning over the kids makes us much more approachable by the adults too."

$410 buys 20 Polaroid film packs.

$24.95 buys a Polaroid 600 instant camera.

How to Help

You can make a donation online, by phone or by check. 100% of your contribution will be used to buy and ship the requested instant cameras and film.

If donating by check, make payable to Spirit of America and write "Snapshot" in the check memo area to make sure your donation is properly allocated.

Contact Information

Spirit of America
12021 Wilshire Blvd., Suite 507
Los Angeles, CA 90025
800-819-7875
staff@spiritofamerica.net
Website: www.spiritofamerica.net
Donations: www.spiritofamerica.net/projects/182

Photo credit: Staff Sgt. William Greeson, USMC

#22

Irrigation Equipment for Helmand Province

SPIRIT OF AMERICA

Summary

You can provide irrigation equipment so the farmers in Khan Neshin can solve their largest problem growing crops.

Description

Less than 25% of lands in Khan Neshin, Helmand Province will be irrigated for farming this year due to lack of water. Lieutenant Colonel Tim Grattan, US Marines, wants to help the drought-devastated farmers in this part of Afghanistan. One part of the solution is solar-powered well pumps being provided by Spirit of America.

LtCol Grattan writes, "We operate in the Southern Helmand area in the Rig District. Rig is comprised of 11 principle villages and several outlying farms. It is a farming area with no formal schools, hospitals, or infrastructure (save a few dirt roads). All in all, it's a pretty rural area dominated by the Helmand River and a series of canals that irrigate the farmland (primarily to the North). Its capital is Khan Neshin. The greatest need here, and the number one concern of residents, is irrigation."

By helping the Marines solve the farmers' irrigation problem you will make an impact in the lives of hundreds of villagers who are struggling to raise life-sustaining crops. If they are successful, the villagers will be able to earn enough money to open schools, support a police force, and resist insurgents for the long term. And, the Marines will have established relationships supportive of their safety and their mission.

HELP THE AFGHAN PEOPLE

$2,150 buys a complete American-made solar-powered well pump.

$65 buys 100 feet of irrigation piping, making an additional field arable.

How to Help

You can make a donation online, by phone or by check. 100% of your contribution will be used to purchase and ship the equipment needed for this and other irrigation projects in Afghanistan.

If donating by check, make the check payable to Spirit of America and write "Irrigation" in the check memo area to make sure your donation is properly allocated.

If your business can donate well pumps or irrigation gear in quantity, please email or call Spirit of America.

Contact Information

Spirit of America
12021 Wilshire Blvd., Suite 507
Los Angeles, CA 90025
800-819-7875
staff@spiritofamerica.net
Website: www.spiritofamerica.net
Donations: www.spiritofamerica.net/projects/190

Photo credit: LtCol Tim Grattan, USMC

#23

Knit Blankets and Clothing for Afghan People

AFGHANS FOR AFGHANS

Summary

You can knit a blanket, sweater, hat or socks for needy citizens of Afghanistan.

Description

Afghans for Afghans is a humanitarian and educational people-to-people project that sends hand-knit and crocheted blankets, ("afghans"), sweaters, vests, hats, mittens, and socks to the beleaguered people of Afghanistan.

This grassroots effort is inspired by Red Cross volunteers who made afghans, socks, slippers, and other items for Soldiers and refugees during World Wars I and II and other times of crisis and need.

A gift of a handmade blanket or garment will bring comfort and warmth to Afghan women, men, and children who continue to suffer from oppression, war, hunger, poverty, and sickness. A gift, made by American hands will send a message of concern and hope to our fellow humans on the other side of the globe.

The organization suggests using the color green in your knits. Green is the symbolic color of Islam. Prophet Muhammad wore a green turban, and green is believed to have been his favorite color. Green was also the color of the banners used on the battlefield and the color of the first Islamic flag.

Islam also considers green significant because it is the color of nature. Therefore, green is popularly used in the flags of Muslim nations, as well as in art and architecture. Mosques are frequently decorated with green tiles.

How to Help

You can make a monetary donation online or by mail through the Agape Foundation. Checks should be made out to "Agape Foundation/afghans for Afghans."

You can knit or crochet something to contribute to an individual afghans for Afghans project.

You can buy an Afghan theme knitting pattern, which supports women's literacy classes in Kabul.

Contact Information

Mail and donations:
afghans for Afghans
P.O. Box 475843
San Francisco, CA 94147-5843

Send knitted items to:
afghans for Afghans
c/o AFSC Collection Center
65 Ninth Street
San Francisco, CA 94103
afghans4Afghans@aol.com
Website: www.afghansforafghans.org

#24

Laptops for Women Writers

AFGHAN WOMEN'S WRITING PROJECT

Summary

You can provide laptops and thumb drives to young Afghan women writers whose voices are traditionally silenced.

Description

You can bring hope and help to young Afghan women whose voices are traditionally silenced, who take enormous risks to write about their lives, and who at times, keep their work secret even from family members. Some have received "night letters" – threats from the Taliban – because of the work they do. They need laptops and thumb drives so they can continue to get their words out into the world, and so we can benefit from hearing those words.

Afghan Women's Writing Project works to free Afghan women from the bonds of silence by providing them with English-writing courses and a safe outlet for their words. The women are given laptops and thumb drives so they can tell their personal stories in online English-writing classes taught by a rotating group of gifted female American poets, novelists, journalists, memoirists and university professors. The teachers nurture the women and encourage them to express their fears, hopes and dreams - something many have never dared to do before.

The project offers three levels of writing workshops with thirty students, and a very long waiting list. Every week the teachers e-mail students a suggested topic. Students e-mail their work back to the teacher to be edited. Many fear retribution if caught and must do their work in secret. With laptops and thumb drives, the women can write in a place they find secure and ask a sympathetic male relative to send their work back to the teachers from an Internet café.

Afghan Women's Writing Project was founded in May 2009 by Masha Hamilton, a successful novelist who first visited Afghanistan in 2004. Masha was awed and inspired by the resolute courage of the women she met.

The project is aimed at allowing Afghan women to have a direct voice in the world, not filtered through male relatives or members of the media. Masha publishes the women's best essays and poems on a blog and in a newsletter, using first names only due to security concerns. Readers are invited to comment, making dialogue possible. The blog never fails to instill a sense of pride in the women, who pour their hearts into their work. It also helps educate the world about the joys and sorrows of Afghan women in today's turbulent world.

Afghan Woman
by Roya
Who asks about my identity?
I am lost on the pages of history books.
Look at my tired face
And the dried tears in my eyes.
My first name is "Afghan woman"
My last name is "Suffer."

How To Help

You can donate online or by mail.

Contact Information

Afghan Women's Writing Project
c/o Masha Hamilton
686 Sterling Place, Brooklyn, New York 11216
masha@mashahamilton.com
Website: http://awwproject.wordpress.com
Donations: http://awwproject.wordpress.com/donations

Photo credit: Kathleen Rafiq

#25

Leadership Skills for Promising Students

GLOBAL FUSION

Summary

You can help Afghanistan's most promising students learn essential leadership skills that will give them the opportunity to become influential forces of change.

Description

Lasting change in Afghanistan will become a reality when the current and future generations of leaders are exposed to and embrace transformational thinking and leadership development. Global Fusion is partnering with the Leadership Development Institute

to provide funding for the expansion of this high-impact model into new cities, short-term faculty to train the English-speaking students, and scholarships for qualified students to attend.

Decades of turmoil in the country have created a massive exodus of intellectual capital. The Leadership Development Institute exists to train and equip emerging Afghan leaders with the knowledge, skills and personal character that will help to transform Afghanistan's people and future.

Endorsed by the University of Herat, the Leadership Development Institute is a one-year long program that teaches proven leadership principles to top students and professionals in academic, business, political and medical spheres. The students, both male and female, are chosen based on a strict admission process. They are referred to the LDI by public, private, and government institutions, and also by the local university.

Global Fusion founder Ross Paterson has been engaged in transformational development work in Afghanistan for the past seven years. He sees the tremendous, untapped potential of these young Afghan students. The money Global Fusion raises helps cover student tuition, staff salaries, training materials, and local (Afghan-based) overhead for the operation.

The graduates from this program have produced six Fulbright scholars, and key leaders all over Western Afghanistan. One student, who has political aspirations to be in the parliament and a future president, said that if he gets elected president he will chose his whole cabinet from the LDI graduates because they are so well trained as leaders. The program has had an immense impact on the students it has helped.

"I believe the LDI has been the first and most productive place ever in Afghanistan that has helped the Afghan youth enhance their capacity in leadership. With the existing high demands for effective leaders in the society and the continuation of the sufferings of this nation due to absence of better leaders, I believe the work by the LDI is just invaluable. From being a self centered person only concerned with his life, I turned into someone passionate to make a positive impact on the lives of the people around me. I started to dream big and envision broader perspectives in my career and life." – S.R., Fulbright Scholar currently studying in the US

How to Help

You can make a donation online or by mailing a check to the address below. If donating by check, put Leadership Development Institute in the memo line.

You can offer to serve on the Global Fusion faculty.

Contact Information

Global Fusion Inc.
6331 Boulevard 26, Suite 250
North Richland Hills, TX 76180
817-874-6161
ross@globalfusion.cc
Website: www.globalfusion.cc
Donations: www.globalfusion.cc/donate.htm

#26

Livestock and Income Skills for Afghan Women

CARE

Summary

You can provide women in Afghanistan with the ability to earn income by selling eggs or milk, allowing them to sustain themselves and their families.

Description

These projects aim to increase the earning capacity of vulnerable women in Afghanistan to become self-sufficient through targeted training activities.

Poultry Development for Women: This project helps vulnerable widows to earn income by providing them with 30 chicks and start-up materials. Widows also learn reading, writing and math skills and how to price and sell eggs. To date, more than 2,500 women have benefited from poultry raising activities.

Widows' Income Generation through Livestock Development (WIGLD): This project helps widows to supplement their families' diets and earn income through animal husbandry. To date, almost 150 widows have received milking cows on credit and have enrolled in Savings and Credit Groups.

These projects are just one of ten programs CARE conducts in Afghanistan.

CARE's mission is to serve individuals and families in the poorest communities in the world.

CARE facilitates lasting change by:

- Strengthening capacity for self-help
- Providing economic opportunity
- Delivering relief in emergencies
- Influencing policy decisions at all levels
- Addressing discrimination in all its forms

CARE places special focus on working alongside poor women because, equipped with the proper resources, women have the power to help whole families and entire communities escape poverty.

How To Help

You can donate online, by phone, or by mail. Reference program AFG020 to help support the Poultry Development for Women and Widow's Income Generation Through Livestock Development (WIGLD).

Contact Information

CARE
Gift Center
PO Box 1871
Merrifield VA 22116-9753
800-422-7385
info@care.org
Website: www.care.org
Donations: www.care.org/donate

#27

Medical Supplies and Hospital Equipment

SPIRIT OF AMERICA

Summary

You can provide critical medical supplies and hospital equipment to needy Afghan clinics and hospitals.

Description

Spirit of America provides equipment and supplies for Afghan clinics and hospitals identified by American military and civilian personnel.

At the request of the Soldiers of Coalition Joint Task Force Phoenix V, Spirit of America provided electrocardiogram machines, blood pressure cuffs, stethoscopes and other equipment for the Ibnisina Emergency Hospital in Kabul.

Brigadier General Douglas A. Pritt wrote, "It is critical we make a difference in the lives of the common citizens of this troubled country. Ultimately making a positive impact in their lives is what will save American lives, and I salute your ongoing efforts to support this."

To help burn victims in Herat, Afghanistan, Melinda Lord, US State Department, wrote, "Anything that will help these burn patients is a blessing. They have nothing but some cream, and bandages and saline IV for the most needy and Tramadol for pain. It is pure triage there. If a victim has no chance, she just gets wrapped in blankets until she dies. So really, everything is a priority." Spirit of America provided a 40 foot container of supplies, pharmaceuticals and burn-care essentials.

Requests like these for medical supplies and equipment to help the Afghan people come to Spirit of America from Americans serving in all parts of Afghanistan. Your contribution will support these requests.

How to Help

You can make a donation online, by phone or by check. 100% of your contribution will be used to purchase medical supplies and equipment and ship them to Afghanistan.

If donating by check, make payable to Spirit of America and write "Health Fund" in the check memo area to make sure your donation is properly allocated.

If your business can donate hospital equipment or medical supplies, please email or call Spirit of America.

Contact Information

Spirit of America
12021 Wilshire Blvd., Suite 507
Los Angeles, CA 90025
800-819-7875
staff@spiritofamerica.net
Website: www.spiritofamerica.net
Donations: www.spiritofamerica.net/projects/68

Photo credit: Melinda Lord

#28

Medical Supplies for Villages

AMERICARES

Summary

You can provide medical assistance to Afghanistan's women and children. Donations provide critically needed medicines and supplies that will equip under-resourced hospitals and rural health centers with the tools they need to help save lives.

Description

Decades of conflict and human rights abuses in Afghanistan have resulted in some of the highest rates of maternal death globally. High mortality rates can be attributed in part to a lack of trained physicians and midwives. Even where doctors and trained midwives are present, however, they frequently lack the

material resources they need to care for expectant mothers and their infants through pregnancy, birth and the post-natal periods.

AmeriCares, through a partnership with Help the Afghan Children (HTAC) and Afghan Health and Development Services (AHDS), delivers medical commodities to Afghanistan several times a year. Humanitarian aid reaches indigent and vulnerable populations served by hospitals, clinics, schools and refugee camps.

AmeriCares sends regular shipments of medicines and medical supplies to Afghanistan supporting primary health care, trauma care, and maternal and child health services throughout the country.

Shipments also include pediatric and adult hygiene kits and personal care and comfort items such as toothbrushes, body lotions and hand sanitizers. To brighten the day of new mothers and children, cases of social items such as baby clothing, booties, blankets and stuffed animals have been sent. Additionally, shipments include medicines and supplies for other health conditions treated by the hospitals including epilepsy, hypertension, and acute musculoskeletal conditions.

Medical professionals at the local hospitals see the impact of these donations firsthand.

"We receive patients in this hospital from all 34 provinces of Afghanistan. Since this is a teaching hospital, we work under 'Ministry of Higher Education' and not under 'Ministry of Public Health.' Therefore, we do not get any share from the health department," said Dr. Kohdamini, Director of Maiwand Hospital Kabul. "AmeriCares donation was very precious for us. We still have some stock left and now we issue these medicines to poor patients only. We are waiting for the next donation from AmeriCares, especially all type of emergency drugs. Our pharmacy shelves are empty and most of the patients comes to this hospital are very poor and cannot buy medicines from the market."

HTAC and AHDS are committed to providing health services "free of politics or partisanship" and, as a result, are the medical providers of preference for many patients living in active conflict zones.

How To Help

The fastest and easiest way to donate to AmeriCares is by making a donation online. You can specify that donations be restricted for AmeriCares' work in Afghanistan.

If you prefer not to give online, AmeriCares welcomes gifts in any amount by whatever method is most convenient for you. Visit their website for alternative donation methods.

Contact Information

AmeriCares
88 Hamilton Avenue
Stamford, CT 06902
800-486-4357
EGudwin@americares.org
Website: www.americares.org
Donations: www.americares.org

Photo credit: Americares

#29

Microloans for Women-Run Businesses

MENNONITE ECONOMIC DEVELOPMENT ASSOCIATES

Summary

You can unleash entrepreneurship in rural Afghanistan by providing women with access to training and microloans to grow food for market.

Description

One of the best ways to address poverty is to invest in women. When women earn extra income, they tend to spend it on food, clothing and schooling for their children. Helping women gain economic capacity is an excellent way to invest in the future of families and communities.

This is why MEDA has a special focus on helping impoverished women in Afghanistan find ways to earn a living. MEDA programs help resilient, hard-working Afghan women unleash their potential.

Women in Afghanistan must struggle against poverty, political unrest and social upheaval. Through education, training and microloans, MEDA helps these women obtain the opportunity they seek: to earn income, help support their families, and gain respect and dignity.

MahJan is just one of many women MEDA has been able to help. After her husband was killed in the war, she went door to door looking for work to support her four children. Then she joined MEDA's Through the Garden Gate (TTGG) project, which helps women improve their kitchen gardens and tiny farms.

TTGG offers women agricultural and business skills training, literacy classes and access to microfinance loans, giving women the opportunity to purchase the seeds, tools and equipment they need.

This program can make a deep, long-lasting impact for more than 2,250 women and their families. About 1,200 women have seen their yields increase up to eight times; many have tripled their incomes.

Earning money filled MahJan with hope.

"I bought a sheep and goat to provide milk for my grandson. Now, I am saving to buy a cow."

In a society where women have limited freedoms, she is earning a living, building skills and gaining respect and dignity.

Mennonite Economic Development Associates (MEDA), based in North America, has offices in the US and Canada. MEDA has been creating business solutions to poverty in the developing world for more than 50 years. MEDA and its partners help more than 2.8 million clients annually.

How to Help

You can donate online, by phone, or by mailing a check to the address below. If you'd like your donation to be earmarked specifically for Afghanistan, mention that when you call or write Afghanistan on your check memo.

Contact Information

MEDA – Mennonite Economic Development Associates
1821 Oregon Pike, Suite 201
Lancaster, PA, 17601-6466
800-665-7026
meda@meda.org
Website: www.meda.org
Donations: www.ican.meda.org

#30

Midwife Training Center

SPIRIT OF AMERICA

Summary

You can provide equipment and supplies needed by graduates of a Midwife Training Center in Paktya Province at request of Major David Gaitonde.

Description

Reports place Afghanistan's infant mortality rate among the highest in the world. Studies cite illiteracy, poverty, malnutrition, poor hygiene and a crippled health-care system as contributing factors to the high death rate for both infants and mothers shortly after or during birth.

One way to combat this troubling situation is to train midwives to provide local care and education to Afghan women. US Army Major David Gaitonde requests your help in providing supplies to a Midwife Training Center in Paktya Province. With your support, Spirit of America will provide the tools the graduating trainees need to help Afghan women and families.

Major Gaitonde writes, "The Midwife Training Center is a two-year program and the ladies do it voluntarily. They do not get a stipend while in the program. They requested some equipment and I have exhausted all of the local channels without finding someone to provide these items. The school would like stethoscopes and blood pressure cuffs for each student (currently 27) that they can take with them when they graduate. I think that is a great idea because these items are a necessity but the women cannot afford to buy them on their own. We will also provide a digital thermometer and delivery kit to each of them. I really believe we can do some good here."

HELP THE AFGHAN PEOPLE

$1000 buys 27 blood pressures cuffs.

$378 buys 27 digital thermometers.

$135 buys 27 pairs of surgical scissors.

How to Help

You can make a donation online, by phone or by check. 100% of your contribution will be used to buy and ship the items requested for the Midwife Training Center.

If donating by check, make payable to Spirit of America and write "Midwives" in the check memo area to make sure your donation is properly allocated.

If you can donate the requested items in quantity, please contact Spirit of America.

Contact Information

Spirit of America
12021 Wilshire Blvd., Suite 507
Los Angeles, CA 90025
800-819-7875
staff@spiritofamerica.net
Website: www.spiritofamerica.net
Donations: www.spiritofamerica.net/projects/181

Photo credit: David Gaitonde

#31

Nutrition Education for Parents

SAVE THE CHILDREN

Summary

You can reduce malnutrition among Afghan children and improve the staggering mortality rate for children under five.

Description

Malnutrition in Afghanistan is widespread. Save the Children's research in Jawzjan Province fights high levels of malnutrition, especially among children under five. Save the Children's health team in Afghanistan is bringing the benefits of its proven and sustainable nutrition rehabilitation program to children in remote, northern reaches of the country.

The "Positive Deviance/Hearth" approach identifies behaviors practiced by families whose children are well-nourished, and then uses this information to teach others about these positive behaviors. The "hearth," or home, is the location for the child-focused nutrition education and rehabilitation sessions.

By teaching and working in collaboration with community health workers and local health clinic staff, the health team improves children's nutrition while building an important foundation of knowledge and skills for their caregivers.

Save the Children initiated a successful PD/Hearth pilot in Jawzjan Province in 2006. In just 18 months, the initiative has been replicated in other villages there and in Faryab Province. The most recent village to benefit from the initiative has been Toghlamast village in remote, southern Faryab, where malnutrition was 69 percent. Early results suggest that Toghlamast's youngest children will do as well as their peers in other nearby villages, and will be on their way to better health and well-being soon.

How to Help

You can make a donation online or by check.

You can donate through a variety of alternative programs, such as American Express point donations, EBay purchases, and matching gift programs. For a complete list of donation methods, visit Save the Children online.

Save the Children also welcomes and encourages both volunteers and policy advocates.

Contact Information

Save the Children
54 Wilton Road
Westport, CT 06880
800-728-3843
twebster@savechildren.org
Website: www.savethechildren.org
Donations: https://secure.savethechildren.org/01/support_now
Volunteer: www.savethechildren.org/get-involved

#32

Parent Literacy Classes

CHURCH WORLD SERVICE

Summary

You can help Afghan moms and dads learn to read.

Description

This program grew out of Church World Service - Pakistan/Afghanistan's Girls' Education Project (GEP). The GEP contributes to an increase in girls' participation in education and an overall improvement in the quality of teaching and learning in primary schools. Through CWS-P/A and its implementing partner, Afghan Development Association (ADA), the project has helped raise the devastatingly low literacy rates in Afghanistan, particularly for women and girls.

This newest project of the GEP includes adult literacy classes in Qarghayi District in Laghman Province, Afghanistan. The classes increase literacy, raise awareness on health and hygiene, and promote knowledge on the importance of education for children. Adults participating in this program are primarily parents and other community members related to the children that will directly benefit from this project.

Parents are selected based on education, leadership qualities, and a willingness to contribute time to the Parent Teacher Committees. Community members participating in the program are identified through the community elders and local Shura members.

Two separate adult literacy classes, one for males and one for females, are held six days a week. Each class has a total of 25 participants, and the lessons cover reading, writing, and math. ADA has also distributed stationery, particularly notebooks and pens, to the participants of these classes.

CWS helps marginalized communities achieve economic prosperity and improve human and social capital through participatory endeavor, which liberates people and enhances their capacities to take control over their lives.

How To Help

You can make a donation by phone or by check. Visit the CWS website for directions on how to wire a donation.

Contact Information

Church World Service
28606 Phillips Street
P.O. Box 968
Elkhart, IN, 46515
800-297-1516
Kabul: cwskabul@hotmail.com
Jalalabad: cwsjalalabad@hotmail.com
Website: www.cwspa.org

#33

Polio Vaccines for Children

THE ROTARY FOUNDATION

HELP THE AFGHAN PEOPLE

Summary

You can help Afghan children receive the polio vaccination and move the world one step closer to eradicating the disease.

Description

After 20 years of hard work, Rotary and its partners are on the brink of eradicating polio, but a strong push is needed now to root it out once and for all. It is a window of opportunity of historic proportion.

Afghanistan's effort to finish polio has succeeded in cornering the virus in the country's southern region, according to a World Health Organization (WHO) report in February. The region is part of a larger zone of virus transmission that includes southern Pakistan.

Strong immunization coverage of children living in the border areas of Afghanistan and Pakistan is critical to both countries' efforts to end polio. "This is a virus that does not respect borders," said Dr. Rudolf Tangermann, a medical officer with WHO's polio eradication initiative, following Afghanistan's National Immunization Days (NIDs) in 2007. "These two countries cannot eradicate polio in isolation."

Afghanistan's March NIDs reached about 6.9 million children. However, fighting between the Taliban and Afghan security forces prevented immunization of all children targeted by the effort.

Vaccinating children and keeping track of who has been immunized is a challenge in a country without a census and where families, especially in the southern region, are constantly on the move to avoid danger. "In the morning you can go in [a village], but in the afternoon you can't," says Dr. Rahmatullah Kamwak, who works in support of WHO efforts in southern Afghanistan.

Nevertheless, courageous volunteers armed with oral polio vaccine do an extraordinary job of finding children and ensuring they are protected against the crippling disease. The volunteers create a kind of mobile medical record as they work, staining children's fingers with colored markers to verify they've received the vaccine and writing notes in chalk on the doors of mud-brick dwellings to indicate households that have been reached.

"[Afghanistan's] polio campaign is nothing short of heroic," says Martin Bell, UNICEF's ambassador for humanitarian emergencies. "It is setting an example to the world of what can be achieved under the most dire circumstances. . . . If Afghans could eradicate polio from their country in a time of war, what could they accomplish in a time of peace?"

How to Help

You can make a monetary donation online or by mail.

You can become a Rotarian and volunteer your time and services for a variety of causes.

Contact Information

The Rotary Foundation
14280 Collections Center Dr.
Chicago, IL 60693
866-976-8279
contact.center@rotary.org
Website: www.rotary.org
Donations: https://riweb.rotaryintl.org/donor_xml/contributionmenu.asp

#34

Prenatal Care and Training for Mothers

CURE INTERNATIONAL

HELP THE AFGHAN PEOPLE

Summary

You can provide critically-needed maternal services to Afghan mothers and their newborn children in Kabul. Without these services, thousands of women would have nowhere to go to safely deliver their baby.

Description

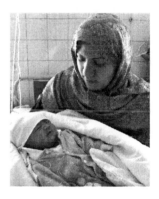

Every hour, two Afghan women die giving birth. Approximately 90 percent of women deliver babies at home without the assistance of a qualified health care worker. Because of the alarming maternal health situation in Afghanistan, prenatal and postnatal health care services to Afghan mothers have become the major focus of CURE's work in Kabul, Afghanistan.

Since 2005, CURE International has operated two medical facilities in Kabul: CURE International Hospital of Kabul and CURE International Family Health Center. Both are dedicated to offering health care to the citizens of Afghanistan.

CURE Kabul gives its patients a chance to deliver their baby in safety, surrounded by the highest-quality equipment and medical staff in the country. CURE Kabul operates a maternity unit for mothers and their newborn children. It also has a modern neonatal intensive care unit to address the needs of critically ill and premature newborns.

Thousands of Afghan women come to CURE's facilities to receive comprehensive prenatal, delivery and postnatal care, regardless of their ability to pay. In fact, more than 9,000 deliveries have been supported through CURE's maternity unit.

Every day in Kabul, the CURE medical team meets the mothers who come to its hospital and family health center in desperate need of a haven to deliver their baby. Their stories are often sad, sometimes unbelievable, but filled with determination and hope.

Shukria's story is a perfect example of the lives CURE Kabul transforms every day. Shukria had suffered through four previous miscarriages. So, when she became pregnant again, she feared that the same thing would happen. This time was different, though. She was able to come to the CURE International Hospital of Kabul for her maternal care. In the expert hands of the hospital staff, Shukria delivered a beautiful, healthy baby. She now knows a happiness she once thought impossible because of CURE Kabul.

"Having worked with CURE International in Kabul for most of the past five years, I have literally seen thousands of mothers and newborns saved as a result of the timely, competent care provided by well-taught midwives and physicians," said Erin Card, Resource Development Director, CURE International. "Last summer I witnessed a young Afghan family shed tears of joy after the successful delivery of its preterm daughter. After numerous unsuccessful pregnancies and miscarriages, how can words adequately describe the joy of a mother and father when they hold their tiny baby for the first time?"

How To Help

You can donate online or by check. Make checks payable to CURE International and write "CURE Kabul" in the memo. Visit the CURE website to find a virtual catalog of services you can sponsor for an Afghan mom and her newborn.

Contact Information

CURE International
701 Bosler Avenue
Lemoyne, Pa. 17043
717-730-6706
info@cureinternational.org
Website: www.helpcurenow.org
Donations: www.helpcurenow.org/motherscatalog

Photo credit: CURE International

#35

Project Afghan Literacy

SPIRIT OF AMERICA

Summary

You can support a literacy program for Afghan men at the request of Army Medic William Seo.

Description

Army Medic William Seo is passionate about helping the people of Afghanistan and is tackling local illiteracy.

He explains, "We started a six-week literacy course, teaching how to read and write Pashto and perform simple math to Afghan Soldiers and local workers. With 76% of illiteracy in Afghanistan, we felt that it is very important to help them learn their language. The first class had 13 students and successfully completed. The graduation was held on August 27, 2009. They never attended any school before and most of them never learned Pashto alphabets. The 50 year-old man even had to be taught how to hold a pencil properly. To our surprise, at the end of 6 weeks, everyone knew how to read and write and even performed addition and subtraction. The students were thrilled. Their commander was so impressed that he made it mandatory for his Soldiers to attend the class. We provide textbooks, notebooks, pencils, erasers, completion certificates, and special awards (most improved, most effort, and the best student award) with prizes.

The literacy program needs notebooks, pencils, erasers, dry markers and erasers for the white board, prizes for the three special awards, and gifts for all of the graduating students."

Spirit of America is providing supplies to support Seo's Project Afghan Literacy.

$600 buys 500 notebooks.

$148 buys 100 packs of erasers.

$84 buys 288 mechanical pencils.

How to Help

You can make a donation online, by phone or by check. 100% of your contribution will be used to buy and ship the items needed to support Project Afghan Literacy and other education requests from Afghanistan.

If donating by check, make payable to Spirit of America and write "Literacy" in the check memo area to make sure your donation is properly allocated.

Contact Information

Spirit of America
12021 Wilshire Blvd., Suite 507
Los Angeles, CA 90025
800-819-7875
staff@spiritofamerica.net
Website: www.spiritofamerica.net
Donations: www.spiritofamerica.net/projects/187

Photo credits: William Seo

#36

Rural Education and Training

NOORISTAN FOUNDATION

Summary

You can help with the development of rural areas of Afghanistan, a key to the country's stability and global security, by supporting schools, midwife training, and providing families with essential items.

Description

The support of the Nooristan Foundation and donors has led to the establishment of the only primary school in the Pasigam village, located in the Nooristan Province of Afghanistan. Nooristan Foundation supports the school by providing teacher salaries, caretakers, rent, backpacks, books, art supplies and locally made tables and chairs.

Classes started on July 1st, 2009. Due to heavy fighting, the roads were closed for many parts of August 2009. Even with these obstacles, significant progress has been made. The Nooristan Foundation hopes that this project will lead to education in areas that have been isolated and have seen conflict and violence over the years. The Foundation believes it can make a difference, one school at a time.

The Foundation is also supporting a program that is training approximately 80 midwives in the Takhar Province of Afghanistan. Afghanistan has one of the worse maternal mortality rates in the world, with approximately 1,600 maternal deaths per 100,000 live births per year. Training is designed to give the midwives practice in a clinical setting and to update and increase their professional knowledge. New classes of midwives who graduate from the program will be able to assist in the delivery of babies and share their knowledge with other midwives.

The Foundation would like to expand the program to another underserved province in the country, where skilled birth attendants are lacking.

With assistance from donors in the US, the Foundation provides essential materials to help families survive in the Baghe Daud camp near Kabul. Each family in the camp has been given plastic sheeting to cover the ground in their shelter; blankets to keep warm; food, including oil, flour, rice, tea, beans, sugar; and coal for fuel and heating. The Foundation believes that once these families are given a chance for a new beginning, they will be able to stand on their own feet.

The Nooristan Foundation was established in 1999, and helped develop programs in the Nooristan Province of Afghanistan. Since then, it has expanded and has provided assistance in other areas of Afghanistan, including Bamiyan, Takhar, Laghman and Kabul. Its purpose is to provide support for charitable and educational projects in rural areas of Afghanistan.

How to Help

You can make a monetary donation online.

You can make a direct donation through Bank of America - Nooristan Foundation Account: 0041-2658-5667.

You can volunteer your time and services. Email Nooristan Foundation at the volunteer email below for more information.

Contact Information

Nooristan Foundation
Great Falls, VA
877-251-9400
info@nooristanfoundation.org
volunteers@nooristanfoundation.org
Website: www.nooristanfoundation.org
Donations: www.nooristanfoundation.org

#37

School Supplies
for Children and Teachers

SPIRIT OF AMERICA

HELP THE AFGHAN PEOPLE

Summary

You can support education in Afghanistan by providing school supplies requested by American troops for Afghan children and teachers.

Description

Spirit of America provides supplies and equipment for Afghan children and teachers at schools identified by American servicemen and women. Some of the supplies in demand are pens, pencils, notebooks, chalkboards, wall maps, microscopes, backpacks and binders.

Here is one example of a school supply request. 1st Lieutenant Roger Chen, US Army, wrote, "The school that I'd like to help is located right between the two small towns of Saturi and Khangukay. The towns themselves are only about a kilometer apart as it is. The towns are in southeastern Afghanistan. This area is very poor and the children there currently have no opportunity to go to school to learn to read, write or do 'arithmetic. The school is very close to being finished but all of the rooms are barren, there are no chalkboards or desks for the students, and obviously no school supplies at this time."

Spirit of America sent school supplies, backpacks and dental kits for the children, as well as wall maps of the world and their country for the schools.

Requests like these for school supplies and equipment to help the Afghan people come to Spirit of America from Americans serving in all parts of Afghanistan. Your contribution will support these requests.

How to Help

You can make a donation online, by phone or by check. 100% of your contribution will be used to buy and ship school supplies and equipment requested by Americans serving in Afghanistan.

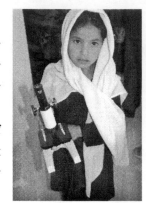

If donating by check, make payable to Spirit of America and write "School Supplies" in the check memo area to make sure your donation is properly allocated.

If your business can donate school supplies in quantity, please contact Spirit of America.

Contact Information

Spirit of America
12021 Wilshire Blvd., Suite 507
Los Angeles, CA 90025
800-819-7875
staff@spiritofamerica.net
Website: www.spiritofamerica.net
Donations: www.spiritofamerica.net/projects/67

Photo credits: Roger Chen, Mark Yaw, Mark Ruiz

#38

Science Center for Afghan High Schools

OPERATION DREAMSEED

HELP THE AFGHAN PEOPLE

Summary

You can help educate Afghan children by providing school supplies and funding for a high school science lab in the southern region of Afghanistan.

Description

Operation Dreamseed is based on the belief that education is a long-term solution to the problems of a generation of children who long for peace, prosperity, security, and freedom. The organization was founded by US Army Major Todd Schmidt as a way of distributing school supplies to children in Afghanistan.

"No chalkboards, no desks, no chalk, no tablets of paper, nothing," said Major Schmidt, recalling the first schoolhouse he saw in Afghanistan. "They're literally sitting in rows on the floor, no glass panes in the windows, drafty schoolhouse that's been gutted. We knew there was a real need here, and if we started providing basic school supplies, we'd be making an impact."

Schmidt saw a way to meet that need by tapping into the generosity of the thousands of Americans who send care packages to the troops.

"We were receiving these care packages," he said. "And everybody that sent us something, we'd send them a note back saying, we truly appreciate your patriotic support for us and what we're doing over here. You don't know us, but you took your time and your energy to contribute this great gift. But if you really, truly are committed to helping us, we'd appreciate if you send school supplies."

This list shows the cost of some items to help you better understand how far your monetary contribution will go, and an idea on what it will be spent. All supplies are purchased in the Afghan economy.

Box of Crayons: $0.15

Lead Pencil Eraser: $0.01

Paper Notebook (80 pgs): $0.90

School Backpack: $5.00

School Desk: $20.00

Teacher's Salary (one month): $50.00

Manual Laborer Wages (per day): $3.00

School lunches (for 100 students for 5 days): $100.00

How to help

You can donate online or by mail. You may indicate that you want your contribution to be used in Afghanistan.

You can donate supplies, time or services. Visit the Operation Dreemseed website for more information.

Contact Information

Operation Dreamseed, Inc.
1 Kimberly Dr.
Rhinebeck, NY 12572
Website: www.operationdreamseed.org
Donations: www.operationdreamseed.org/donate

#39

Self-Sufficiency and Small Business Help for Afghan Women

CATHOLIC RELIEF SERVICES

Summary

You can help Afghan women learn how to care for and feed their families.

Description

In Afghanistan, impoverished women help their families escape hunger through Catholic Relief Services (CRS) self-help programs. This report by Laura Sheahen, CRS' regional information officer for Asia, shows the immense impact the organization's programs have:

"My son was 5. He was so thin," said Khaire Nesa, a 38-year-old Afghan woman. "He died."

Khaire Nesa leads a women's self-help group in the remote Afghan town of Chaghcharan. Khaire can buy more food for her six children because she joined a women's self-help group supported by Catholic Relief Services. In villages across Afghanistan, the groups bring together women who want to earn money. CRS helps them start small home-based businesses, giving them training and supplies like sewing machines.

In a remote town called Chaghcharan, Khaire's group began by raising chickens and selling eggs, but soon took on a larger venture. "There's no bakery in Chaghcharan," said Khaire, so the 20 women decided to start making cakes and cookies to sell.

CRS provided two ovens housed in a domed, mud-wall hut. CRS also gave the women's group flour, cooking oil, baking powder and raisins.

"CRS gave us ingredients for three months. We used it all in 10 days," Khaire said.

After giving out free samples, the bakery quickly got a standing order to provide more than 800 pounds of baked goods every week to the local police. The women also got contracts with two shopkeepers in the local marketplace. In less than two months the bakery was self-sufficient.

The $8-a-week profit each woman takes home is a substantial sum in the impoverished town. For Khaire, whose husband works in one of the town's two gas stations, the money makes a huge difference.

"Three years ago we didn't have enough money for the children and house. We used to eat mainly tea and bread," said Khaire. "Now that I'm part of the self-help group, we have more money. We can eat rice, yogurt and meat."

Khaire says that the bakery earnings have translated into more respect for the women at home.

"One woman's husband is disabled, he can't work. He would beat his wife, and one time he threw a scalding cup of tea at her," said Khaire. "Now they are happy because the woman is earning money. He stopped the violence."

How to Help

You can help in many ways, including a one-time online donation, monthly giving, and a gift catalogue.

Contact Information

Catholic Relief Services
228 W. Lexington St.
Baltimore, Maryland 21201-3413
888-277-7575
info@crs.org
Website: www.crs.org
Donations: https://crs.org/donate

#40

Sewing Machines for Afghan Women

SPIRIT OF AMERICA

Summary

You can provide sewing machines and sewing supplies to Afghan women who will use the equipment to earn a living and clothe their families.

Description

Spirit of America responds to requests from Americans serving in Afghanistan for sewing machines and supplies to help local women.

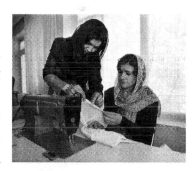

Spirit of America provided sewing machines to the Marines for women's sewing centers in Ramadi and Fallujah, Iraq. The sewing centers provided a place where local women could earn a living and develop the confidence needed to begin participating in local affairs. This was a program that gave heart as it changed minds.

Marine General James Mattis wrote, "The sewing centers are getting good use and more are planned. We should see a lot of very beneficial impact as the word of these spread. While the first one in Ramadi is well attended, I am surprised at even greater anticipated use in smaller, less affluent areas. Thank you and your team again."

With increasing stability and the ability to engage in more meaningful economic development in Afghanistan, Spirit of America anticipates sewing machine requests like the one from Marines in Ramadi.

Requests like these for sewing machines help the Afghan people come to Spirit of America from Americans serving in all parts of Afghanistan. Your contribution will support these requests.

How to Help

You can make a donation online, by phone or by check. 100% of your contribution will be used to buy and ship sewing machines and supplies requested by Americans serving in Afghanistan for the benefit of local Afghan women.

If donating by check, make payable to Spirit of America and write "Sewing Machines" in the check memo area to make sure your donation is properly allocated.

If your business can donate sewing machines or supplies, please email or call Spirit of America.

Contact Information

Spirit of America
12021 Wilshire Blvd., Suite 507
Los Angeles, CA 90025
800-819-7875
staff@spiritofamerica.net
Webite: www.spiritofamerica.net
Donation: www.spiritofamerica.net/projects/74

Photo credits: Getty Images; US Marine Corps

#41

Shoes and Sandals for Children

SPIRIT OF AMERICA

Summary

You can provide shoes and sandals for Afghan children that are requested by American servicemen and women.

Description

Many Afghan children do not have anything to wear on their feet. Others have only open-toed sandals which aren't adequate during the cold winter months.

Spirit of America provides shoes and sandals for Afghan children at the request of American troops in Afghanistan.

Army Sergeant James Baker wrote, "Every day we roll outside the wire we see kids and adults in need of the basic necessities. We've been seeing this for 12 months now. But today was especially troubling to me and one of my Soldiers. The temperature today was a low of 18 and a high 25. That's not including the wind chill factor. During our short convoy of only a few miles we saw at least four children with open toed sandals and no socks on standing in the snow waving as we passed. Later we saw two other young kids with socks and no shoes running in the snow to catch up to our convoy. If you have any means of helping out, please do so. These kids really do need whatever you can afford to send."

Spirit of America sent 164 pairs of Teva sneakers and 240 pairs of socks to Sergeant Baker. Army Chaplain Abe Dispennette asked for children's sandals and Spirit of America provided 100 pairs.

Chaplain Dispennette wrote, "I wish I could explain how excited those kids are to get something like sandals. It's like giving a kid in the States an XBox."

Army Medic William Seo is very active in humanitarian efforts in Afghanistan. One of his goals is to help Afghan girls.

Seo wrote, "We are committed to provide 200 elementary school children with a pair of running shoes."

Your contribution will support requests like these. This is an opportunity to help our troops put shoes on the feet of Afghan children who need them.

How to Help

You can make a donation online, by phone or by check. 100% of your contribution will be used to buy and ship shoes and sandals for Afghan children that are requested by Americans serving in Afghanistan.

If donating by check, make payable to Spirit of America and write "Children's Shoes" in the check memo area to make sure your donation is properly allocated.

If your business can donate shoes or sandals, please contact Spirit of America.

Contact Information

Spirit of America
12021 Wilshire Blvd., Suite 507, Los Angeles, CA 90025
800-819-7875
staff@spiritofamerica.net
Website: www.spiritofamerica.net
Donations: www.spiritofamerica.net/projects/196

Photo Credits: SGT. Andre Reynolds; William Seo

#42

Small Business Loans for Women

MERCY CORPS

Summary

You can provide women in Afghanistan with small business loans and financial products to help them grow their businesses. These efforts help reduce poverty and generate employment opportunities for women.

Description

Ariana Financial Services is one of the first microfinance institutions (MFI) in Afghanistan, providing small loans that clients are using to open or grow a small business in all areas of economic life – from weaving to carpentry to food processing.

Started in 2003 by Mercy Corps, Ariana is now a self-sustaining MFI helping women become more self-sufficient through small business entrepreneurship. Since its launch, Ariana has supported more than 16,900 clients with a total of approximately $3.2 million in loans. Eighty-two percent have been women.

Lending to women improves the lives of entire households. Women spend their extra earnings on food, education and other necessities for their families. Microfinance helps women, who in turn build stronger, healthier families and communities.

Nasrin is a great example of how these small loans can change lives. She lives in northern Kabul where she supports her four children by baking naan and bolani bread to sell in her neighborhood. Her bakery exists thanks to a small loan from Ariana Financial Services with which she bought flour, wooden spatulas and pays for maintenance on her oven. Nasrin is on her fourth loan with Ariana. With each loan, both her business and her home life have improved. She is planning on expanding her business by setting up a second oven, which will allow her daughter to enter the business and help sell more bread to better support the family.

Storai Sadat, a former Mercy Corps employee, now Executive Director of Ariana Financial Services explains, "The Taliban had a very bad effect on women's mindset in Afghanistan. Even after they left, many women doubted their ability to work and make a living after having been confined to their homes for six years. The reason for Ariana's focus on female clients is cultural. In Afghanistan, women take on a large part of the responsibility of caring for the family. It is a question of honor for them to repay any debt they might have. Afghan women simply are far more unlikely to default on a debt than men are."

How to Help

You can donate online to Mercy Corps to support programs like Ariana Financial Services.

You can also take action through the Mercy Corps Action Center at www.actioncenter.org.

Contact Information

Mercy Corps
Department NR, PO Box 2669
Portland, OR 97208
800-852-2100
info@mercycorps.org
Website: www.mercycorps.org
Donations: https://donate.mercycorps.org

Photo Credit: Miguel Samper for Mercy Corps

#43

Soccer Balls for Kids

KICK FOR NICK

Summary

You can provide soccer balls and soccer equipment to Afghan children so they can enjoy being children.

Description

Kick for Nick sends soccer balls and equipment directly to service members who then distribute the sports equipment to the local children. This program provides the children with the opportunity for constructive play, and also helps the service members to secure positive relationships with the local population.

Soldiers who have distributed the balls to the children have reported that this act of kindness and generosity has given way to an atmosphere of friendship and camaraderie. The ball distribution, a gesture of friendship regardless of political differences, brings a feeling of hope and unification - leaving no room for cultural or religious barriers.

The initial idea to donate soccer equipment came from Private First Class Nicholas Madaras. Nick's love for soccer started early on, and he became a devoted youth coach. Soon after graduating high school he was deployed to Iraq, and he was amazed at how well the children there played soccer. He asked his father to send over any old balls he could find.

While on leave from Iraq in 2006, Nick rounded up as many soccer balls as possible to bring back to the children near his post. Being a passionate soccer player himself, Nick felt that this gesture of good will would bring happiness to numerous children. Tragically, Nick was killed by an IED before he was able to distribute the balls himself. He was only 19 years old.

Shortly after Nick's passing, Ken Dartley contacted Nick's parents after reading about Nick's passion for the sport, and his desire to share this love with the Iraqi children, in a newspaper article. Ken, a Korean War veteran himself, wanted to start a program of collecting soccer balls to fulfill the crusade that Nick has started.

What started as a local soccer ball drive has now expanded across the country. Thousands of balls have been received from 45 of the 50 states. The Kick for Nick Foundation sends soccer balls to Afghanistan, Iraq and other places where American servicemen and women request them.

Each ball that is send overseas has one thing in common – PFC Nick Madaras is written on each one. While Nick is no longer with us, his spirit and his legacy lives on in the hearts of the children who continue to play soccer thanks to an effort Nick started.

How To Help

You can make a donation online.

You can also donate soccer balls and equipment, or organize a ball collection drive. Visit Kick for Nick online for details.

Contact Information

Kick For Nick Foundation
c/o Bill Madaras
35 Signal Hill Road South
Wilton, CT. 06897
203-563-0013
madintl@aol.com
Website: www.kickfornick.org
Donations: www.kickfornick.org/support-kickfornick

Photo credit: Kick for Nick Foundation

#44

Solar-Powered Radios for Remote Villages

SPIRIT OF AMERICA

Summary

You can help open communication and open minds in remote villages by donating solar- and hand-crank-powered radios.

Description

The Taliban attempts to isolate and intimidate Afghan villagers. The Marines seek to connect and inform them, and to do so have requested solar- and hand-crank-powered radios.

Marines 1st Lieutenant Mike Kuiper explains, "The Taliban continue to prevent the people from being educated, keep the people in fear, and do anything they can to gain power."

Radios will help the Marines by providing Afghans a connection to the outside world and better information. Spirit of America will provide radios to Marines in Nawa, Helmand Province, and to other Americans serving in Afghanistan who request them to give as gifts to local Afghans.

Lieutenant Kuiper gives more background on the need, "The radios you are providing give the people of Nawa a chance to hear what is going on in the world. Right now the only way they hear news is by word of mouth or through the local Mullahs, who are sometimes illiterate. With radios they can hear that the government is working, and are less likely to join the Taliban and kill American forces. Support such as with Spirit of America is vital in convincing the people that we are not enemies of Afghanistan, but friends. This is the way we will win.

"Radios pick up signals from Nawa itself, and some from Lashkagah and farther. Radios will help them stay in touch with the world more. The governor does radio addresses, we advertise wheat distribution, fertilizer distribution, etc, and it gives them some entertainment while they work. There are a few villages that aren't as friendly to us as others, and we would like to distribute them there. Every single radio you send us will absolutely help win the hearts and minds of Nawa, and also allow them to get information that dispels Taliban lies."

This is a way to help open isolated areas of Afghanistan to the outside world and to support American service members.

How to Help

You can make a donation online, by phone or by check. 100% of your contribution will be used to buy and ship radios requested by Americans serving in Afghanistan to provide to local people.

If donating by check, make payable to Spirit of America and write "Radios" in the check memo area to make sure your donation is properly allocated.

Contact Information

Spirit of America
12021 Wilshire Blvd., Suite 507
Los Angeles, CA 90025
800-819-7875
staff@spiritofamerica.net
Website: www.spiritofamerica.net
Donations: www.spiritofamerica.net/projects/183

Photo credit: SSgt William Greeson, USMC

#45

Sponsor an Afghan Woman

WOMEN FOR WOMEN INTERNATIONAL

Summary

You can help an Afghan woman rebuild her life through financial and emotional support.

Description

Women for Women International's Sponsorship program creates a unique experience by building a one-to-one relationship between you and a woman who lives thousands of miles away in Afghanistan.

By sponsoring a woman you not only provide her with the financial assistance she needs to get back on her feet, but also the hope and emotional support that are the keys to rebuilding her life after war.

As a sponsor, you will be matched with a woman in Afghanistan. Your monthly contribution will provide her with rights awareness education and job skills training so she can continue to support her family in the future. She will also receive a portion of your contribution in direct aid so she can provide her family with basic necessities.

Each sponsor receives a welcome kit with the name of the woman they are sponsoring, and her background information – Does she have children? Is she married? She learns your name too, because until she is matched with you, she cannot begin the program.

You will be able to exchange letters. In fact, your letters are a powerful tool for helping a woman in this war-torn country know that there is someone out there who knows of her existence amd cares enough to sponsor her and write to her. Many women in the program have never received a letter addressed to them, so it is a large boost to their self-esteem.

Not only do your monthly donations and your letters help Aghan women, but your connection with them can change your life too. Many sponsors feel they unexpectedly "get" far more than they receive. You'll be astounded at the strength and courage these women have in the face of so much adversity.

A sponsored woman in Afghanistan receives:

- Emotional support and encouragement from her trainers, fellow participants and from you, her sponsor
- Training on leadership, rights awareness and the role of women in society
- Job skills training applicable to the local economy
- A network of women to connect with in her community
- Small business assistance
- Infant care classes in Afghanistan

How to Help

You can make a monetary donation online.

You can start the sponsorship process online, and may indicate Afghanistan as your country of choice.

Contact Information

Women for Women International
4455 Connecticut Ave NW, Suite 200
Washington DC 20008
202-737-7705
sponsorship@womenforwomen.org
Website: www.womenforwomen.org
Donations and Sponsorships: www.womenforwomen.org

#46

Sponsor an Orphan

INTERNATIONAL ORPHAN CARE

Summary

You can sponsor a child to provide his/her education, nourishment, health care, hygiene education, and recreation.

Description

In Afghanistan, seventy percent of men and nearly ninety percent of women are illiterate. The country also has the world's highest rate of mortality for pregnant women, with more than twenty percent of Afghan children dying before the age of five. International Orphan Care is trying to battle these depressing statistics.

International Orphan Care (IOC) began operations in Jalalabad in 1993 to provide vocational education for orphans. IOC's mission is HOPE - to Help Orphans be Productive and Educated – for a better tomorrow.

For $25/month, you can sponsor an orphan in Afghanistan and provide the essential programs a child needs to develop and thrive. Each center provides education, meals, hygiene assistance, clothing, vocational training, recreational activities and guidance primarily for orphaned children ages 5 to 13 years old.

International Orphan Care's outreach changes the lives of orphans and provides them with HOPE. Mike Whipple, IOC Chairman and CEO, encountered a great example of that when he visited Jalalabad in 2007:

"I met a young man who had attended IOC's school in the 1990's. He had returned to the school to deliver some food, clothing and school supplies, to help the current students who like him came to the school after losing a parent.

"When he was a child, his father had been murdered while visiting the Mosque. Shortly after his father's death, his family home was bombed. His mother, two brothers and a sister moved to Jalalabad to live with his uncle and his uncle's children."

"The boy wanted to continue his studies and learn English but his uncle told him that the family could not afford the expense of school supplies and English lessons. When the boy told his teacher that he could not pay to attend school, his teacher told him that there was another school in Jalalabad that was free for orphans."

"The boy came to the IOC school and after some discussion was allowed to join the classes. At the end of the school day, he returned home to tell his family that he was learning English, he received books, paper, pencils and a free lunch, and after classes the boys played volleyball."

"Today the boy and his eldest brother work as interpreters earning much more than what the average Afghan earns. The youngest brother is studying to be a doctor and is a member of the Afghanistan's National Volleyball Team training to compete in the Olympics."

How To Help

You can make a donation online, by phone, or by check.

Volunteer opportunities are available to travel abroad to teach at IOC schools, as well as help plan, organize and implement events to raise awareness and funds.

Contact Information

International Orphan Care
P. O. Box 3397
Laguna Hills, CA 92654-3397
949-939-1712
info@orphanproject.org
Website: www.orphanproject.org
Donations: www.orphanproject.org/donations.html

Photo credit: International Orphan Care

#47

Sponsor Education for Children in Poverty

CHILD FOUNDATION

Summary

You can provide basic needs and supplies for a child and his or her family including food, clothing, school supplies, birthday gifts, and monthly financial assistance.

Description

Child Foundation's mission is to help children living in poverty to remain in school. The children sponsored through the programs are high achievers, but many of the children are orphans or children living in emergency situations. By receiving an education, the children

are able to move beyond the stigma of poverty and gain the tools they need to reach their true and full potential.

Because each child's needs are unique, a social worker is assigned to work with the family to determine the best ways to help. Some families receive food, such as bulk supplies of rice, pasta, oil, tea, or sugar. Some children are given clothing, including school uniforms. School supplies, such as backpacks, notebooks and textbooks, are another common need.

In an area where many people live off of less than $1.00 a day, monthly financial assistance can also prove invaluable. With the financial burden lightened, it is often easier for children to attend school.

Child Foundation has sponsored more than 3,000 children to date, with 60% of the children being girls. The impact sponsorship can have on the life of a child can be seen in the story of Banafsha, a young girl living in poverty in Kabul.

Banafsha, a twelve-year-old girl living in a poor area of Kabul, had been acting as the breadwinner for her family by selling gum to support her siblings, mother, and drug-addicted father. She was aware that the streets of Kabul were far from safe, and while most girls her age dream of more extravagant fantasies, Banafsha dreamed of being able to go to school. Child Foundation assigned a social worker in Kabul for Banafsha and then her family received a sponsor.

Through assistance from Child Foundation and her sponsor, Banafsha is now enrolled in school and has reached the 2nd grade level. She has a tutor to help her with her studies. Her family has food on their table and Banafsha has new clothing and supplies for school. Now that Banafsha can concentrate on school instead of merely surviving, she dreams of completing her education and someday becoming a teacher.

How To Help

You can make a donation in any amount online, by phone, or by mailing a check to the address below.

You can also sponsor a specific child for as little as $20/month. You can choose a child from the Child Waiting List, or simply check the Afghanistan box when signing up online. By phone, you may ask about available Afghan children. When donating by check, write "For Afghanistan" in the memo.

Contact Information

Child Foundation
1220 SW Morrison Street, Suite #500
Portland, OR 97205
503-698-4084
cfmain@childfoundation.org
Website: www.childfoundation.org
Donations: www.childfoundation.org

#48

Surplus Medical Supplies for Hospitals

MEDSHARE

Summary

You can provide hospitals in developing countries with the life-saving medical supplies and equipment they require to treat people in need.

Description

MedShare is an organization dedicated to bridging the gap between surplus and need through the recovery and redistribution of surplus medical supplies and equipment from healthcare institutions to those most in need.

MedShare collects surplus medical supplies and equipment from hospitals, medical companies and individuals, and then redistributes them to needy hospitals in developing countries. The organization only accepts unused, unexpired medical supplies. All biomedical equipment donations that are used are later refurbished by the organization's biomedical engineers.

Donated medical supplies are sorted and repackaged by trained volunteers and are then entered into an online inventory database. Qualified health recipients abroad can custom-order the specific medical supplies their facility needs. The custom-ordered medical supplies and equipment are then shipped to the recipients in forty-foot shipping containers.

Since its inception in 1998, MedShare has shipped 500 forty-foot containers of surplus medical supplies and equipment to 80 countries in the developing world.

In 2009, MedShare shipped a 40-foot container of medical supplies and equipment, sponsored by the nonprofit organization American Medical Overseas Relief (AMOR), to Afshar Hospital, a new medical facility in Kabul, Afghanistan. The supplies and equipment were collected from 20 Northern California hospitals through MedShare's innovative medical surplus recovery program. The medical aid shipment provided more than 800 boxes of vitally-needed supplies such as surgical gloves, IV sets and sutures. MedShare also sent a portable ultrasound, an X-ray unit and surgical lights.

"Rather than go into landfills, these donated medical supplies and equipment will have a second chance to save lives in war-torn Afghanistan. We are excited to join AMOR in their endeavors to improve the quality of life in this country," said Chuck Haupt, Executive Director of MedShare's Western Region.

Afshar Hosptial will use the donated medical supplies and equipment to primarily focus on maternal care and pediatrics. It will also provide urgent care, general medical services, immunizations and essential medicines.

How to Help

You can make a monetary donation online. Donations can be earmarked for specific shipment projects. You can also sponsor a forty-foot container.

You can donate unused, unexpired medical products.

You can volunteer to help sort and repackage donated medical supplies at the Atlanta and San Francisco locations.

Contact Information

MedShare National Headquarters
3240 Clifton Springs Road
Decatur, GA 30034
770-323-5858
info@medshare.org
volunteer@medshare.org
Website: www.medshare.org
Donations: www.medshare.org/donate

#49

Toys and Sporting Goods for Children

SPIRIT OF AMERICA

HELP THE AFGHAN PEOPLE

Summary

You can brighten the lives of Afghan children with toys and sporting goods that are requested by Americans serving in Afghanistan.

Description

Many Americans serving in Afghanistan seek opportunities to do nice things for Afghan children. Often the requests are for small gifts, such as toys or sports equipment, that the children can play with. These help both the children and the troops.

Sergeant Major Mack McDowell asked for stuffed animals, Frisbees and jump ropes. 1st Lieutenant Mike Kuiper asked for puzzles, soccer balls and nets, and volleyballs and nets. Rachel Hudak requested plastic jewelry for girls.

Army Chaplain Abe Dispennette, who requested soccer balls, wrote, "I'm a Chaplain stationed in Afghanistan. I am currently working on a humanitarian effort to get soccer balls to some of the poorer children in the area just outside my base here. I would love all of your help! Soccer is a cheap sport that all the children here love to participate in, and I would love for all of to be a part in giving them something to take their mind off of some of the awful things that go on here. So please help me, send some soccer balls here so we can get rolling on this effort. Thank you all so much for your love and support to all of us."

Spirit of America gets many requests for toys and sporting goods from Americans serving in all parts of Afghanistan. Your contribution will support these requests. This is an opportunity to put smiles on the faces of many Afghan children.

How to Help

You can make a donation online, by phone or by check. 100% of your contribution will be used to buy and ship toys and sporting goods for Afghan children requested by Americans serving in Afghanistan.

If donating by check, make payable to Spirit of America and write "Toys/Sports" in the check memo area to make sure your donation is properly allocated.

If your business can donate toys or sporting goods, please contact Spirit of America.

Contact Information

Spirit of America
12021 Wilshire Blvd., Suite 507
Los Angeles, CA 90025
800-819-7875
staff@spiritofamerica.net
Website: www.spiritofamerica.net
Donations: www.spiritofamerica.net/projects/67

Photo credit: MC1 Monica R. Nelson, US Navy; James McDowell

#50

Trees and Crops for Farmers

GLOBAL PARTNERSHIP FOR AFGHANISTAN

Summary

You can help Afghan farmers support themselves and their communities with crops and fruit- and nut-bearing trees.

Description

Two decades of war have brought almost unparalleled destruction to Afghanistan. The land can no longer support the bountiful agriculture that once sustained 80% of Afghans, accounted for 50% of the country's GDP, and made Afghanistan self-sufficient in food production.

Global Partnership for Afghanistan (GPFA) is helping Afghan farmers who are striving to help themselves. GPFA provides these historically self-reliant people the opportunity to lift their families out of poverty and restore economic and environmental sustainability to their country.

GPFA's community-based programs have provided Afghan men and women with the planting supplies, tools and training they need to revitalize and rebuild the vast network of farmer-owned fruit nurseries, orchards, vineyards and woodlots that have long formed the backbone of Afghanistan's economy. With an established presence in central Afghanistan, GPFA is expanding its operations province by province to help ensure a secure, prosperous and healthy future for farm families throughout the country.

GPFA works to help rural Afghans revive and rehabilitate their fruit and nut orchards, vineyards, croplands and forests, thereby generating food, jobs, income, and environmental and health benefits. Depending on local conditions and needs, GPFA's support combines two or three distinct types of plantings:

- Fruits and vegetables to harvest within a year

- Saplings and root stock to restore orchards and vineyards within three to five years
- Trees for reforestation to replenish topsoil, diminish erosion and provide economic benefits

The Guldara District suffered greatly from war and the resulting destruction. When the fighting came to this cluster of villages, residents were forced to flee as the Taliban forces burned virtually everything, leaving only the damaged mud-brick shells of their homes. Each day, deminers add large white check marks to village buildings, indicating that new territories are free of dangerous land mines and safe for activity.

GPFA and local community leaders launched demonstration projects in the Guldara District in 2004 aimed at increasing food security and generating income. Now encompassing some 70,000 trees, these projects are designed to integrate local skills, resources and conditions and achieve rapid financial sustainability for broad replication across Afghanistan.

Orchards are typically intercropped with annual vegetables and herbs in the first two years, providing an immediate source of food and income. The project is expected to produce from fruit sales a net family income of $1,000 - $2,000 annually after 3-5 years, with higher rates expected as the orchards fully mature.

How to Help

You can donate online or my mail. If donating by mail, you will need to download a donation form from the GPFA website and send it with your check to the mailing address below.

Contact Information

Global Partnership for Afghanistan
P.O. Box 1237
New York, NY 10276-1237
212-735-2080
info@gpfa.org
Website: www.gpfa.org
Donations: www.gpfa.org

#51

Water Well Construction

AFGHAN CARE TODAY

Summary

You can provide clean, safe water for Afghan children who would otherwise be forced to walk miles to find fresh water.

Description

Afghan Care Today (ACT) has teamed with Global Water Partners, which has committed the initial funds necessary to drill numerous water wells that ACT will oversee in remote locations of Afghanistan. There is a current need for $75,000 in operational funds to send a qualified team and the proper equipment to Afghanistan in order to implement the water well project.

ACT will initially drill a well for an orphanage of blind Afghan children who must walk more than two miles to obtain fresh water. As part of this project, ACT will also provide medical care with the donated medicines and medical supplies that they currently have palletized and ready for shipment from the United States.

Few healthcare providers, regardless of how well traveled, have visited foreign hospitals, evaluated its supplies and examined the training regimen of its medical staff. ACT is culturally-sensitive and experienced at working side-by-side with host nation people, frequently in their own language.

ACT was launched in late 2008 by former members of the US Army Special Forces Group (A) to provide humanitarian assistance to the people of Afghanistan. They are professionals, with full-time careers ranging from aerospace engineering to medical device sales, who volunteer their time and personal finances in order to help the Afghan people.

How to Help

If you are interested in making a donation, call or email ACT.

Contact Information

Afghan Care Today
3700 State Hwy 35 N
Port Lavaca, Texas 77979
979-229-3193
info@afghancaretoday.com
Website: www.afghancaretoday.org

#52

Wheelchairs for the Injured and Disabled

SPIRIT OF AMERICA

Summary

You can provide wheelchairs requested by American troops for injured and disabled Afghan children and adults.

Description

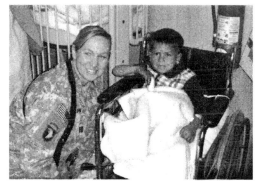

Afghans who need wheelchairs often cannot afford to buy them. And, many Afghan hospitals are not equipped to meet the need. Spirit of America has provided wheelchairs for Afghans at the request of American Soldiers and Marines.

Army Eric Ruthman explains the need, "There are many land mines left over from military activity in the area prior to US and Coalition forces arriving. The children who are injured by mines are treated at the Egyptian hospital near Bagram Airfield and need the chairs to help them as they heal and learn to cope with life after their mine accident. Many of these children have lost limbs. The chairs provide them with the mobility they need and improve their quality of life immensely.

"These efforts help the children which is the primary and most important reason I am doing this. But there are other second order effects. Afghan adults, parents, friends and family of these children see us helping them which enhances feelings of good will toward US and Coalition forces who are working very hard to help Afghanistan as a sovereign nation."

Spirit of America also provided wheelchairs requested by Army Major Terri Selph. She wrote, "These wheelchairs will improve the quality of life immensely for the Afghan people who have lost limbs due to land mine accidents. I met an 11-year old boy who also was injured by a land mine. He lost his right arm and had significant injuries on his back and side. This little boy was more concerned about his grandfather receiving a new pair of shoes."

"It's truly amazing what the Afghan people overcome on a daily basis. They are kind and generous and are extremely grateful for the donations they receive. They have touched me. Thank you again for your contributions and for making a significant difference in the lives of the Afghan people."

Spirit of America receives requests for wheelchairs for injured Afghans from Americans serving throughout Afghanistan, most recently from Marines in Helmand Province. Your contribution will support these requests and provide needed wheelchairs.

How to Help

You can make a donation online, by phone or by check. 100% of your contribution will be used to buy and ship requested wheelchairs.

If donating by check, make payable to Spirit of America and write "Wheelchairs" in the memo area to make sure your donation is properly allocated.

Contact Information

Spirit of America
12021 Wilshire Blvd., Suite 507
Los Angeles, CA 90025
800-819-7875
staff@spiritofamerica.net
Website: www.spiritofamerica.net
Donations: www.spiritofamerica.net/projects/192

Photo credit: Terri Selph

#53

"It's On Me"

RANDOM ACTS OF KINDNESS

Summary

You can surprise a service member with an unexpected gift, such as a coffee, beer, or burger, as a thank you for their service and sacrifice.

Description

The men and women of our military devote themselves to serving America and protecting our freedoms. Saying thank you is always appreciated, but sometimes you'd like to do more. When you see a service member in an airport or standing in line for a cup of coffee, surprise them with a random act of kindness.

How To Help

When you see a service member ready to purchase something like a cup of coffee, a newspaper, or tank of gas, step in and offer to pick up the tab. Or if you are ahead of them in line, you can tell the cashier that you'd also like to pay for their order.

Most stores have gift cards. Purchase one, hand it over to the service person and tell them that it's on you.

If you own a business, consider offering a discount to service members. The gesture is a great way to say thank you for serving our country.

Many organizations provide opportunities to make purchases that will be sent to the troops. Green Beans Coffee's Cup of Joe program lets you send a hot cup of coffee and note of encouragement to Soldiers overseas. Six Packs for Soldier encourages people to upload a photo of themselves toasting the troops, and in return sends a beer to a deployed service member.

Keep your eyes open in your community for similar opportunities.

HELP THOSE WHO SERVE

Contact Information

Green Beans Coffee – Cup of Joe: www.greenbeanscoffee.com/coj/
Six Packs for Soldiers: www.sixpacksforsoldiers.com

#54

Adaptive Clothing for Injured Service Members

SEW MUCH COMFORT

Summary

You can provide adaptive clothing to support the unique needs of wounded service members from all branches of the military and National Guard.

Description

Each week, wounded military members arrive in the United States from Germany for extensive medical treatment for bullet wounds, burns, head and limb injuries and amputations. These injuries require large prosthetics and casts that are too bulky to fit under ordinary clothing and underwear. Sew Much Comfort is the only organization providing adaptive clothing at no cost to our wounded service members. Without adaptive clothing the only option for them is a hospital gown.

Founded in 2004, Sew Much Comfort has distributed more than 90,000 adaptive garments and comfort accessories. The organiza-tion ships to any location where wounded service members are recovering from their injuries.

The driving force behind the success of the Sew Much Comfort organization is its 1600 volunteers that span the United States, Canada and Europe. All of the garments are designed to be completely opened either right side, left side or both sides (double) using Velcro openings. This allows for ease of dressing and provides ready access to the injury or wound area by the service member, medical staff or family. The clothing also allows injured service members to easily dress themselves, and their clothing appears as normal as civilian attire which helps facilitate a more natural and comfortable recovery.

HELP THOSE WHO SERVE

One grateful mother of a wounded service member writes, "A HUGE thank you for the amazing work you are doing for our injured heroes!!! Our son broke his right elbow and left wrist in Iraq, and was flown to Walter Reed Army Medical Center for surgeries... Our son wanted some "real" shirts to wear while recovering, and we were so happy when someone brought a care package of your adapted shirts to his room. Our son was thankful for something to fit over his casts so he could look "normal" while he recovered!!!"

"Aside from the practical use of the shirts, I can't begin to describe the boost it gave emotionally to know someone cares. When theses young men and women realize their health, career, and entire future looks like it may be altered drastically, simply having a need met lifts the spirits more than words can describe."

How To Help

You can donate online by visiting the Sew Much Comfort website. You can also sign up to hold a fundraiser or clothing drive.

Contact Information

Sew Much Comfort
13805 Frontier Lane
Burnsville, MN 55337
michele@sewmuchcomfort.org

Distribution Facility:
6655 Lookout Road #101
Boulder, CO 80301-3371
smcdistro@sewmuchcomfort.org
Website: www.sewmuchcomfort.org
Donations: www.sewmuchcomfort.org/

Photo credit: Sew Much Comfort

#55

Adaptive Technology for Injured Service Members

SOLDIERS' ANGELS

Summary

You can provide laptops and other technology for severely-wounded service members to help with their physical and psychological recovery.

Description

One of many projects run by Soldiers' Angels, Project Valour-IT provides voice-controlled/adaptive laptop computers and other technology to support Soldiers, Sailors, Airmen and Marines recovering from severe injuries.

Donations go towards the purchase of the following recovery tools:

Voice-controlled Laptops - Operated by speaking into a microphone or using other adaptive technologies, they allow the wounded to maintain connections with the rest of the world during recovery.

Wii Video Game Systems - Whole-body game systems increase motivation and speed recovery when used under the guidance of physical therapists in therapy sessions. The systems are donated to medical facilities so all wounded Soldiers may benefit from the technology.

Personal GPS - Handheld GPS devices build self-confidence and independence by compensating for short-term memory loss and directional challenges related to severe TBI and severe PTSD.

A Lieutenant Colonel had this to say about his recovery with the help of Valour-IT, "I was thrilled and truly appreciative of the laptop donation that Soldiers' Angels sent. My neurology team is ecstatic with the progress that I have made, yet we all temper our excitement as I still have a long recovery ahead. Due to the great hearts (sponsors, donors, volunteers and others too numerous to mention) within Soldiers' Angels I have become more mobile in

HELP THOSE WHO SERVE

my rehabilitation and the laptop is absolutely one of the tools that I have in my recovery toolbox. I use it to keep current on my schedule and have several applications that assist with recovery."

How To Help

You may make a monetary contribution online by debit or credit card. Checks can be mailed to the address below.

Valour-IT also allows individuals or groups to sponsor the recovery of an individual Soldier. Visit Soldier' Angels online to be paired with an injured Soldier on the waiting list.

Contact Information

Project Valour-IT
Soldiers' Angels
1792 E. Washington Blvd
Pasadena, CA 91104
626-529-5114
Web site: www.soldiersangels.org/project-valour-it.html
Donation: www.soldiersangels.org/valour-it-donations.html

#56

Adopt a Soldier

SOLDIERS' ANGELS

Summary

You can provide personalized aid and comfort to a member of the United States Army, Marines, Navy, Air Force, or Coast Guard by sending letters and care packages during his/her deployment.

Description

For deployed service members, kind words from home can make all the difference. Getting regular correspondence reminds the brave men and women of our country that they have support. By choosing to "adopt" a Soldier, you are paired one-on-one with a deployed service member, and you have the unique opportunity to make a connection.

You can sign-up to adopt a Soldier on the Soldiers' Angels website. Once approved, you will receive an email with all the information about your adoptee that is available. The information you receive is provided by the adoptee directly, a family/friend of the adoptee, or someone in the adoptee's unit. You can get additional information about your adoptee by simply asking him/her in your first letter.

When you adopt a Soldier, you agree to send at least one letter a week and one care package each month during the duration of the deployment. Adopted Soldiers know that they will receive a personal letter each week from someone who sat down to write the letter just for them. Care packages bring deployed service members some of the small comforts of home. Some of the most commonly requested items include gum, books, sunscreen, small snacks and candy, toothpaste, and calling cards. Soldiers' Angels also sells pre-made care packages that they will ship directly for you.

While hundreds of thousands of letters and care packages have been sent to-date, there are still service members waiting to be adopted. The best way to illustrate the powerful way these letters and packages make a difference is through the worlds of the service members they have helped.

A grateful Soldier in Afghanistan wrote, "I would love to thank everyone at Soldiers' Angels… I know that when mail call came around and they called my name, my day was instantly better, and I'm glad that there are people out there that are willing to write and send things. It boosted my morale and made it easier. The time flew by because I got books and snacks and a lot of other things. Thank you very much from the bottom of my heart."

MG Peter W. Chiarelli wrote, "I am convinced that these accomplishments would not have been possible without fabulous contributions such as yours. Not only were these gestures sincerely appreciated, but they rallied the morale of the Soldiers, often at the most necessary times, and were absolutely critical to our mission completion. In other words, we could not have done it without you!"

How to Help

You can sign-up on the Soldiers' Angels website to adopt a Soldier. Once approved, you will receive all of the information you need to make a connection with your service member.

If you know of a service member who would benefit from being adopted, visit Soldiers' Angels online to submit their information.

Contact Information

Soldiers' Angels
1792 E. Washington Blvd
Pasadena, CA 91104
626-529-5114
Website: http://soldiersangels.org
Adopt a soldier: http://soldiersangels.org/join-soldiers-angels.html
Request for adoption: http://soldiersangels.org/submit-a-soldier.html

#57

Assistance for Injured Marines

INJURED MARINE SEMPER FI FUND

Summary

You can provide financial assistance and quality-of-life solutions for injured Marines.

Description

When Marines, Sailors, and other military personnel assigned to Marine Forces, are injured or critically ill, their entire family shares the pain and burden of recovery. Normal life is put on hold, often times for weeks, months, or years, as loved ones travel great distances, at a moment's notice, and stay at the bedside. They take leave from their jobs, often without pay, and incur additional expenses for childcare, lodging, travel, specialized equipment, and other necessities. Few families are prepared for the expenses they face. They need help, and they need it quickly. The Injured Marine Semper Fi Fund was created to meet this need.

The Injured Marine Semper Fi Fund provides financial assistance and quality-of-life solutions for Marines, Sailors and other military personnel assigned to Marine Forces, injured in post 9-11 combat, training, or with life-threatening illnesses, and their families. The fund provides relief for immediate financial needs that arise during hospitalization and recovery as well as perpetuating needs such as home modifications, customized transportation and specialized equipment.

The Injured Marine Semper Fi Fund was established in May 2004. A nurse at the Camp Pendleton Naval Hospital, whose husband was deployed to Iraq, saw first hand the needs of those returning from battle. She brought together a group of Marine Corps spouses with diverse backgrounds to implement a plan to provide financial grants to OEF/OIF injured Marines, Sailors, and service members injured while assigned to Marine forces, and their families during their difficult road to recovery.

A Governing Board of retired Generals and Officers, Senior Enlisted Marines, and others with professional backgrounds was added to help the Fund develop into a nationwide program. The Fund works closely with the Marine Corps, the Navy, and military hospitals nationwide to identify and assess the needs of OEF/ OIF specific families. The Fund depends on the generosity and compassion of people from all walks of life to join the quest of "serving those who preserve our freedom."

How to Help

You can make a monetary donation online or by mail. Checks should be accompanied by a donation form that can be found online.

For alternative donation programs, such as corporate matching, monthly donation programs and honorary donations, visit the Semper Fi Fund website.

Contact Information

Injured Marine Semper Fi Fund
825 College Blvd, Suite 102
PMB 609
Oceanside, CA 92057
703-640-0181
Website: www.semperfifund.org
Donations: www.semperfifund.org/donate.html

#58

Assistance for Injured Special Operations Personnel

SPECIAL OPERATIONS WARRIOR FOUNDATION

Summary

You can provide financial assistance to severely injured special operations personnel and their families so they can be together as the service member recovers.

Description

The Special Operations Warrior Foundation provides immediate financial assistance to special operations personnel severely wounded in the global war on terror. Once notified of a special operations Soldier, Airman, Sailor or Marine hospitalized with a severe injury, the Special Operations Warrior Foundation immediately sends funds to the service member (or his/her designated recipient) so the family and loved ones can travel to be bedside.

To date, the Special Operations Warrior Foundation has provided more than $800,000 to wounded special operations personnel.

"At the Special Operations Warrior Foundation, we are extremely thankful for the support provided by the Gulf Coast Community Foundation. With the Foundation's $500,000 grant, we are able to provide immediate funds enabling family members to travel and be at the bedside of their loved one as soon as humanly possible. The expenses involved can be overwhelming for families of the wounded, but thanks to your wonderful generosity we are able to assist deserving families in time of need," said Colonel John T. Carney Jr. (Ret.), president/CEO of Special Operations Warrior Foundation.

The Special Operations Warrior Foundation also provides full educational scholarships, not grants, for surviving children of fallen Army, Navy, Air Force and Marine Corps special operations personnel. Funding includes tuition, books,

HELP THOSE WHO SERVE

fees, room and board. Today, there are some 125 students enrolled in colleges and universities across the country with funding from the Foundation. The foundation has seen 152 of its college students graduate.

How To Help

You can make a donation online or by check. You can also contribute through the Combined Federal Campaign (CFC # 11455).

Visit the Special Operations Warrior Foundation website for other ways to give, such as donating your vehicle or arranging planned giving.

Contact Information

Special Operations Warrior Foundation
P.O. Box 13483
Tampa, FL 33681
813-805-9400
Website: www.specialops.org
Donations: www.specialops.org

#59

Assistance for Returning Troops

OPERATION HOMEFRONT

Summary

You can provide emergency and morale assistance for our troops, the families they leave behind and for wounded warriors when they return home.

Description

When a service member deploys overseas to defend our freedom, they leave behind a family who loves and supports them. However, the family is seldom fully prepared for what this service and sacrifice entails. Often, the deployed service member was the one who repaired the car, balanced the checkbook, fixed the refrigerator when it acted up, or helped every evening when it's was time to read a bedtime story or change a diaper.

Operation Homefront makes a difference in the lives of military families. The organization leads more than 4,500 volunteers in 30 chapters nationwide and has met more than 105,000 needs of military families. Additionally, Operation Homefront hosts a web community for military spouses called Operation Homefront Online.

Operation Homefront believes the military "has our back," so the organization strives to make certain we "have their backs" here at home. The organization meets the needs of military families when they are in crisis and when they have nowhere else to turn. It serves the junior enlisted families of active duty, activated guard and activated reserve of all five uniformed service.

HELP THOSE WHO SERVE

Whether it's rent, mortgage, utilities, car payments, car repairs, groceries or medical expenses which exceed insurance or emergency food assistance, Operation Homefront helps families so their service member overseas is secure in knowing there is assistance in their absence.

Examples of the great work done by Operation Homefront are everywhere. One poignant example came when an Army Specialist and his wife suffered a tragedy that no family should ever endure. Like many wives of wounded service members, this wife was the glue for her family after her husband was injured by an IED for the fifth time. He was evacuated from Iraq back to the United States where he was diagnosed with post-traumatic stress disorder and a traumatic brain injury. The wife and their three children made several long trips to be with their husband and father as he recovered. On one of their many road trips, a gust of wind caused the wife to lose control of their SUV. The vehicle rolled four times, killing two of their children instantly. Their third son died three weeks later. Operation Homefront helped this family with financial assistance, getting them qualified for Social Security benefits, finding a lender to help them buy a home, and provided furniture donations for their new house.

How To Help

You can make a donation online, by phone, by check or by participating in a State Giving or the Combined Federal Campaign (CFC). You can choose to donate on the national level or directly to your local Operation Homefront Chapter.

You can donate gift cards from food stores and major retailers.

You can volunteer your time at your local chapter. To find the chapter closest to you, visit the Operation Homefront website.

Contact Information

Operation Homefront
8930 Fourwinds Drive, Ste. 340
San Antonio, TX 78239
800-722-6098
info@operationhomefront.net
Website: www.operationhomefront.net
Donations: www.operationhomefront.net/donate.htm

#60

Building Homes for Injured Service Members

BUILDING HOMES FOR HEROES

Summary

You can help build or refurbish homes for injured service members and their families.

Description

Building Homes for Heroes was created to provide a way for individuals, groups and corporations to assist the severely injured and disabled men and women of the United States Military, and their families, as they begin their struggle with post-war life. Service members can come home badly burned, with permanent disfigurements, missing limbs, the loss of sight or ability to walk, psychiatric conditions or paralysis.

For the severely wounded and disabled, each day is a struggle to cope with the life-altering injuries they've sustained. For those returning to civilian life that are blind, confined to a wheelchair or severely burned, activities we take for granted such as bathing, cooking, reaching cabinets and getting in and out of bed are arduous tasks. Building Homes  for Heroes helps to lift the burden by providing housing at little or no cost to the injured veterans.

Building Homes for Heroes is composed of a diverse group united by a common bond: a strong commitment to the men and women of the military who put their lives on the line to protect us and ensure our freedom. The idea began in 2005, when while driving to work, the founder heard severely wounded Soldiers speaking on the radio and pulled over to hear the inspiring words these

HELP THOSE WHO SERVE

young men had to offer. He called the radio station to make a donation.

From there, a small group got together and talked openly about finding ways to make a significant difference in the lives of wounded Iraq and Afghanistan war veterans and their families. They made the decision to form an organization that would improve the quality of life for our heroes through various means. Many service members return from the war in need of home repairs, major renovations, modifications, and in some cases brand new homes tailored to their special needs.

Building Homes for Heroes carries out fundraising activities such as golf outings, 5K runs, t-shirt sales, and awareness nights. It also participates in military appreciation events to raise funds to provide special military families with new homes, or renovations/ modifications to existing homes.

With the help of volunteers and generous donations, Building Homes for Heroes has been able to provide some very special American heroes, and their families, with the help they deserve as they return to civilian life.

How to Help

Donations can be made online, over the phone by credit card, or by sending a check to the address below.

To inquire about volunteering your time and talent at an event, or about hosting an event, contact Building Homes for Heroes.

Contact Information

Building Homes for Heroes
65 Roosevelt Avenue
Valley Stream, NY 11581
516-684-9220
info@buildinghomesforheroes.org
Website: www.buildinghomesforheroes.org
Donations: www.buildinghomesforheroes.org/donate.htm

#61

Calling Cards for Soldiers

CELL PHONES FOR SOLDIERS

Summary

You can donate your retired cell phone and have it exchanged for calling cards that are sent to deployed troops so they can call their loved ones.

Description

Each year, millions of people in the United States replace their old cell phones. Now, those old phones can become a valuable gift for deployed service members. Cell Phones for Soldiers, with the help of thousands of volunteers all across the country, collects retired cell phones and exchanges them for calling cards so deployed service members can call their loved ones for free.

Every donated cell phone provides approximately 60 minutes of talk time, and the recycling of the old phones are beneficial for the environment. There are nearly 40,000 drop-off points across the country where you can donate your old phone. You can also go online and print a shipping label and mail your phone in.

The simple act of donating an old cell phone can make a large difference. For our service members abroad, phone calls home can be the morale boost they need to keep going.

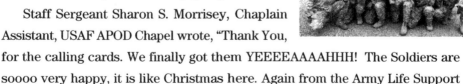

Staff Sergeant Sharon S. Morrisey, Chaplain Assistant, USAF APOD Chapel wrote, "Thank You, for the calling cards. We finally got them YEEEEAAAAHHH! The Soldiers are soooo very happy, it is like Christmas here. Again from the Army Life Support Area …Thank You."

Cell Phones for Soldiers was founded in 2004 by teenagers Robbie and Brittany Bergquist with just $21 of their own money. Since then, the organization

HELP THOSE WHO SERVE

has raised nearly $2 million in donations and distributed more than 500,000 prepaid calling cards to Soldiers serving overseas.

"Cell Phones for Soldiers started as a small way to show our family's appreciation for the men and women who have sacrificed the day-to-day contact with their own families to serve in the US armed forces," said the teens' father, Bob Bergquist. "Over the past few years, we have been overwhelmed by the generosity of others. But, we have also seen the need to support our troops continue to grow as more troops are sent overseas for longer assignments."

How to Help

You can make a monetary donation in any amount online or by phone.

You can donate your old cell phone by visiting Cell Phones for Soldiers online and searching for the nearest drop-off location, or printing a shipping label.

To become a collection point, and find out more about helping provide communications for our deployed warriors, visit the Cell Phones for Soldiers website.

If you would like to request a calling card for a deployed service member, visit Cell Phones for Soldiers online.

Contact Information

Cell Phones for Soldiers
c/o The Bergquist family
243 Winter Street
Norwell, MA 02061

Cell Phone Recycling Address:
2555 Bishop Circle West
Dexter, MI 48130
800-426-1031
cellphonesforsoldiers@recellular.com
Website: www.cellphonesforsoldiers.com
Donations: www.cellphonesforsoldiers.com/donatemoney.html

#62

Camo Quilts

AMERICAN LEGION

Summary

You can send service members handmade quilts that will provide comfort and warmth while they are deployed abroad.

Description

The Camo Quilt Project, which has sent out more than 2,100 quilts to service members headed overseas, started in 2006 when Linda Wieck's son-in-law asked her to knit him a quilt that he could take to Iraq for his deployment. His request was simple: just a blanket that was small, camouflage, made with cotton batting and ideal for a first deployment.

That summer, when Todd was training in Camp Shelby, Miss., the 48 Soldiers in his unit noticed the quilt and expressed interest in having one. Wieck promptly made a quilt for all of them and shipped them to Camp Shelby before they deployed in July 2006. It was a modest beginning for the Camo Quilt Project, which started as a small volunteer effort in Plymouth, Wisc., but ballooned into something much greater as media of all sizes began reporting on it. Three and a half years later, Wieck and hundreds of volunteers have sent out an estimated 2,175 quilts to service members from as far away as Germany. They've received financial backing and donations from all over, and a local company – Glacier Transit & Storage – gave office space to her and her volunteers to use.

"I really enjoy doing this," Wieck said. "I love to sew. When my son-in-law asked for one and I found there was a demand for them, I decided this is what I'm going to do."

Service members from all branches can request a quilt. They're told how much it costs to produce and can choose to donate whatever amount they want. Costs are kept low because of donations and because Wieck buys fabrics from a thrift supplier on the east coast.

"Some (service members) give a little bit because that's all they have. Some give hundreds of dollars," Wieck said.

Donations for quilts are sent to Franklin Post 387 in Plymouth. The American Legion facilitates the funds to Wieck and her volunteers, and the quilts are produced and shipped out. Many of the project's volunteers are from the Legion family.

"The American Legion is my sponsor," Wieck says. "All my funds go through The American Legion. They have been on board with me since day one."

How to Help

You can make a monetary donation by mailing a check to the address below.

You can donate other items needed to make the quilts faster and more efficiently. Visit the Camo Quilts website for the items most needed.

Contact Information

Camo Quilts
Franklin Legion Post 387
c/o Steven Bender
N7417 Bittersweet Rd
Plymouth, WI 53073
920-627-3460
linda.camoquilt@gmail.com
Website: http://camoquiltproject.blogspot.com

American Legion – National Headquarters
Website: www.legion.org
Donations: www.legion.org/donate

#63

Care Packages

OPERATION GRATITUDE

Summary

You can lift morale and put smiles on faces by sending care packages and letters addressed to individual Soldiers, Sailors, Airmen and Marines deployed overseas.

Description

Operation Gratitude care packages contain food, hygiene products, entertainment items and personal letters of appreciation, all wrapped with good wishes of love and support.

Tens of thousands of American Service Members are deployed in hostile and remote regions of the world, including the Middle East, Afghanistan, and on ships throughout international waters. The physical conditions they must endure are difficult and they may be separated from loved ones for long periods of time.

Through collection drives, letter writing campaigns and donations of funds for shipping expenses, you can express your respect and appreciation to the men and women of the US Military in an active, hands-on manner.

Some of the donated items placed in the care packages may include: Beanie Babies/Webkinz, Girl Scout Cookies, sunscreen, gum, candy, phone cards, batteries, DVDs, CDs, socks and personalized letters of thanks.

Families may request online that a care package be sent to their loved one in the military. Operation Gratitude then contacts the deployed service member requesting their full roster so every person in the unit will receive their own package.

In January, 2009, the District of Columbia's premier service event, "A Day of Service for Our Military," was a partnership between Operation Gratitude,

Target and Serve DC, providing participants the opportunity to express their appreciation to those who serve our nation in uniform. Volunteers gathered inside a heated tent at RFK stadium to assemble care kits for inclusion in the Operation Gratitude care packages to be shipped during the year. First Lady Michelle Obama, Dr. Jill Biden and 25 members of Congress joined 12,000 Operation Gratitude volunteers to assemble an astounding 85,000 care kits.

Perhaps the impact is best described by Major General Mark Hertling, "What kind of difference has it made? Our Commanders made it a point to visit every single battalion and brigade during the three days surrounding Christmas. In every location, I saw numerous Operation Gratitude packages. Every Soldier received a personalized note, some holiday cheer, and some treats. And you know what? It wasn't the gifts or the cards or the notes that made such an impression...it was the realization that someone cared about our Soldiers as individuals, understood the importance of their mission and appreciated their sacrifice."

How to Help

There are several ways to get involved. You can donate financially by mail or online. You can organize a fundraising event or a collection drive in your area. And you can write and collect letters of thanks that will be added to the care packages.

Contact Operation Gratitude to learn more about the items that are needed, and acceptable, for the packages that help our men and women in uniform.

Contact Information

Operation Gratitude
16444 Refugio Road
Encino, California 91436 USA
818-909-0039
info@OpGratitude.com
Website: www.OperationGratitude.com
Donations: www.operationgratitude.com
How to Help: www.opgratitude.com/howtohelp.php
To Request Care Packages: www.opgratitude.com/packages.php

Photo credit: Operation Gratitude

#64

Career Assistance for Returning Service Members

HIRE A HERO

Summary

You can mentor and/or find work for returning service members.

Description

In 2006, the Armed Forces Support Foundation was created, along with Hire A Hero, to provide free employment services to returning service members and their families. Hire A Hero is an online professional networking site that provides employment services specifically geared towards meeting the employment needs of returning military members and their families.

Conventional job boards fail to address the specific needs of returning veterans and do not connect the veterans with the wider military community. Hire a Hero is a national program that was created to address this gap.

Hire a Hero began as a professional networking website focused on employment as returning service members transition from military to civilian life. The organization's mission is to serve the greater military community by providing an international accessible online community that creates job opportunities for returning veterans. Hire A Hero provides access to meaningful employment and connects veterans to mentors.

Hire A Hero has grown into a nation-wide resource that connects unemployed veterans with job opportunities, education, training, social services, and counseling with the goal of providing consistent support throughout the veteran's career. Hire a Hero has been able to help many veterans find careers. These placement achievements are based on using web 2.0 professional networking technology that creates a platform to allow the veterans to connect with other veterans.

Hire a Hero's successful approach was recognized by Time Magazine as one of the top 21 ways to "Fix America" and was ranked at number 11.

How to Help

You can make a monetary donation online.

If you were an active service member, you can become a mentor and help today's returning men and women develop a career in civilian life. Register online at the Hire a Hero website.

Contact Information

Hire A Hero
Armed Forces Support Foundation
5245 College Avenue, Suite 408
Oakland, CA 94618
866-447-3243
Website: www.hireahero.org
Donations: www.hireahero.org/donations

#65

Donate Airline Miles

FISHER HOUSE FOUNDATION: HERO MILES

Summary

You can help injured service members recovering at military and VA hospitals reunite with their families by donating your frequent flier miles.

Description

Hero Miles reunites families at the bedside of service members wounded in Iraq or Afghanistan. It also helps family members who need to travel to their homes or jobs and back to the medical facility.

Hero Miles assists Military Mortuary Affairs Teams with travel for specific family members not able to receive military assistance to attend the funerals of service members killed in Iraq or Afghanistan.

The program is comprised of individual airlines whose passengers donate their frequent flyer miles to assist service members and their families. Donated miles go to support airline tickets for hospitalized service members, medically approved to leave a military or VA hospital for a visit home and return, who don't qualify for convalescent leave or other government funded travel. If the service member is unable to leave the hospital, tickets are provided to their families and close friends to enable them to be at the bedside of their loved one.

Hero Miles has provided more than 18,000 tickets to hospitalized service members and their families, worth nearly $25 million. The average savings per ticket is approximately $1,300.

For the injured men and women of our military, the support of family and friends can make all the difference in their recovery. Below is a letter of appreciation from a family who received airline tickets from Hero Miles.

HELP THOSE WHO SERVE

"I would like to say 'thank you' for allowing my son and I the chance to return home for a visit. We are currently at Walter Reed Army Medical Center and through your 'Hero Miles' program we were finally able to return home for a brief rest after having been here for 11 months. My son was wounded in Iraq exactly a year ago this week and has undergone many surgeries and procedures. He is still recuperating but has come such a long way."

"Thanks to 'Hero Miles' our trip was worry-free and short, since we were fortunate to have a direct flight and this all made for a much easier and more enjoyable break."

"Thank you again so much. We just wanted to let you know how much we truly appreciate all that you do, not just for us, but for all the military families."

"Sincerely,

The Stephen Family"

How to Help

You can donate your frequent flyer miles from participating airlines to Hero Miles. A current list of participating airlines and specific directions for donating can be found online.

Contact Information

Fisher House Foundation: Hero Miles
111 Rockville Pike, Suite 420
Rockville, MD 20850
301-294-8560
info@fisherhouse.org
Website: www.fisherhouse.org
Donations: www.fisherhouse.org/programs/heroMilesDonate

Photo credit: Fisher House

#66

Emergency Messages to Families of Troops

RED CROSS

Summary

You can provide financial assistance and facilitate communication between service members and their families during personal emergencies.

Description

Using the latest technology, the Red Cross allows military members stationed all over the world to send messages to loved ones back home during emergencies and other important events.

Red Cross volunteers brief departing service members and their families regarding available support services and explain how the Red Cross may assist them during deployment. Both active duty and community-based military can count on the Red Cross to provide emergency communications that link them with their families back home and provide access to financial assistance and counseling.

American Red Cross communication services keep military personnel in touch with their families following the death or serious illness of a family member or other important events, such as the birth of a child. The information or verification in a message assists the service member's commanding officer in making a decision regarding emergency leave.

The Red Cross also works with the military aid societies: Army Emergency Relief, Navy Marine Corps Relief Society, Air Force Aid Society and the Coast Guard Mutual Assistance. These partnerships help to provide financial assistance in the form of grants or no-interest loans. This assistance may be used for emergency travel, the burial of a loved one or basic needs such as food, temporary lodging, urgent medical needs and funds needed to avoid eviction, utility shut off, etc.

HELP THOSE WHO SERVE

In addition, the Red Cross offers confidential services to all military personnel, including active duty, National Guard and Reserves and their families. Counseling, guidance, information, referrals and other social services are available through a worldwide network of chapters and offices on military installations.

As more and more National Guard and Reserve units are called to full-time duty status, counseling is becoming increasingly important to prepare the Guardsman and Reservists and their family members for the period of activation. Because members of the National Guard and Reserve typically live in civilian neighborhoods, they and their families frequently have difficulty accessing much-needed, military-related social services.

Service members can also request a guide especially for military personnel returning home to their families after a lengthy deployment. The guide has suggestions for making the transition smoother for the entire family.

How To Help

You can make a donation online, by phone, or by mailing a check to the address below. If you wish to donate specifically to Service to Armed Forces, please make a note at the time of donation.

You can volunteer at your local chapter. Visit the American Red Cross website to locate the nearest chapter.

Contact Information

American Red Cross - Mid-Michigan Chapter
P.O. Box 30101
Lansing MI 48909-30101
517-702-3325
thickey@midmichiganredcross.org
Website: www.midmichiganredcross.org

American Red Cross – National Headquarters
2025 E Street NW
Washington, DC 20006
800-733-2767
Website: www.redcross.org
Donate: www.redcross.org/en/donatemoney
Volunteer: www.redcross.org/en/volunteertime

#67

Entertainment and Communications for Troops

USO

Summary

You can help the USO bring a touch of home to our men and women in Afghanistan.

Description

Since before World War II, the USO has been the bridge between the American people and our men and women in uniform, conveying the heartfelt appreciation and support of a grateful nation. Whether it is a quiet place to go for rest and relaxation, movies refreshments, or a friendly face, the USO delivers special service to the military.

To support troops participating in Operations Enduring Freedom and Iraqi Freedom, USO centers opened in Afghanistan, Iraq, Kuwait and Qatar. The USO provides a variety of programs and services, including orientation programs, family events, travel assistance, free Internet and e-mail access, and recreation services. A new program called "USO in a Box" delivers program materials ranging from DVD players and videos to musical instruments to remote forward operating bases in Afghanistan and Iraq.

The USO is also providing services for the annual "Tribute to the Troops" special of World Wrestling Entertainment. They have aired WWE RAW from Afghanistan and Iraq every Christmas in the United States in a pre-taped show from the combat zone.

Military personnel and family members visited USO centers more than 5.3 million times last year. Services include free Internet and e-mail access, libraries and reading rooms, housing assistance, family crisis counseling, support groups, game rooms and nursery facilities.

HELP THOSE WHO SERVE

How to Help

You can make a donation online or by mail. You can designate your contribution to the USO center in Afghanistan.

You can volunteer in a variety of ways, all aimed at helping American service members. Visit the USO website to check out the Locations Directory for more information.

Contact Information

USO World Headquarters
Department WS
PO Box 96860
Washington, DC 20090-6860
800-876-7469
Website: www.uso.org
Donations: www.uso.org/donate
Volunteers: www.uso.org/howtohelp/becomeavolunteer

#68

Helmet Padding Upgrades

OPERATION HELMET

Summary

You can provide deployed and soon-to-be deployed service members with helmet upgrade kits that mitigate head trauma.

Description

Many of the helmets used by service members were designed to protect primarily against bullets and explosive fragments. Through a simple upgrade, these helmets can better protect service members against impact concussions that they face in bomb blasts and motor vehicle accidents.

The helmet upgrades do three primary things:

Protection - Shock-absorbing pads keep the helmet from slapping the skull when hit with blast forces, fragments, or being tumbled along the ground or inside a vehicle. This decreases the chance of brain injury from IEDs, bombs, RPGs, vehicle accidents, and falls.

Comfort - If the helmet is more comfortable, the service member is more likely to keep the helmet on longer and more often.

Stability - Keeps the helmet firmly on the head and out of the eyes.

Service members from all branches of the military have sent their thanks for the helmet upgrades.

A Lieutenant Colonel in the US Air Force wrote, "Thank you for the helmet pads and relief from the pressure and pain associated with wearing the helmets for extended periods of time. The new pads made a difference immediately and allowed me to focus on our convoy mission and not my aching head. I now focus on keeping my team safe outside the wire and not helmets that hurt. Again, your generosity is greatly appreciated by those of us forward. Nice to know we are cared for by outstanding Americans."

A grateful Marine mother wrote, "I recently requested upgrade kits on behalf of my son's squad of 12. They received them within 10 days and are THRILLED with the difference it has made! Now, on behalf of the rest of the Kilo Co, 2nd Plt, I am respectfully requesting that kits be sent to the remaining two squads and the leaders. Kyle has the OK to distribute them to the rest of the platoon as soon as he receives them! These kits make all the difference on a long patrol outside the wire!"

A US Sailor wrote, "I am dumbfounded, speechless, and thankful all at once! I cannot believe that you were able to turn around my order so quickly. From everyone here at DCMA Balad, THANK YOU!"

How To Help

You can donate online through the OPERATION HELMET website. 99.96% of all contributions are used to send upgrade kits to our troops. Donations can be earmarked specifically for Afghanistan, or a specific service or unit on the donation form.

You can also help by volunteering to get the word out to others. Visit OPERA-TION HELMET online to learn about other ways to help, such as organizing fundraisers and writing to your elected officials.

Contact Information

OPERATION HELMET
c/o Dr. Bob Meaders
74 Greenview Street
Montgomery, TX 77356
ophelm@operation-helmet.org
936-449-9706
Website: www.operation-helmet.org
Donations: www.operation-helmet.org/contribute.html
Volunteers: www.operation-helmet.org/getinvolved.html
Request a Kit: http://operation-helmet.org/Kitrequest.html

Photo credit: Operation Helmet

#69

Help End Veterans Homelessness

CIRCLE OF FRIENDS FOR AMERICAN VETERANS

Summary

You can help homeless veterans find work and homes.

Description

Every day an estimated 200,000 veterans sleep unsheltered on the streets of America. Previously the vast majority of these vets had come home from the Vietnam War. Today the ranks of homeless veterans include returnees from Iraq and Afghanistan. Many of these newest veterans return home in need of mental health help. Circle of Friends helps these veterans.

The Circle of Friends for American Veterans is a 501(c)3 designated non-profit organization dedicated to raising awareness about veterans issues, particularly homeless veterans, by influencing public opinion to shape public policy. The Circle of Friends for American Veterans, and its allied publication, the VETERANS' VISION, have provided and continues to provide advocacy for those who deserve it the most and have it the least by conducting nationwide rallies, holding receptions with policymakers and providing direct financial support to transitional facilities that assist homeless veterans.

The Circle of Friends for American Veterans has written modest checks for more than 25 transitional facilities with a disciplined format for otherwise homeless Veterans. Veterans must be drug- and alcohol-free, well groomed, and willing to work. The success rate of such facilities is well over 50%, setting a high standard that gets Veterans back into society where they belong. Marshalling its expertise and creativeness, the Circle of Friends for American Veterans has been able to multiply support for transitional facilities for homeless Veterans.

HELP THOSE WHO SERVE

The long term objective of The Circle of Friends for American Veterans is to lead a national charge to get 50,000 homeless veterans off the streets each year in 2009, 2010 and 2011. This will reduce the number of homeless veterans in America by half and get motivated homeless veterans, willing and able to work, back into society where they belong.

How to Help

You can make a monetary donation online.

Contact Information

Circle of Friends for American Veterans
210 East Broad Street Suite 202
Falls Church, VA 22046
800-528-5385
Website: www.vetsvision.org
Donations: www.vetsvision.org

#70

Home Comforts for Troops

OPERATION: CARE AND COMFORT

Summary

You can provide support and comfort to units of deployed US military service members, serving in Iraq, Afghanistan, and other regions of conflict, by sending letters and packages.

Description

Operation: Care and Comfort, an all volunteer program, exists to provide support and comfort to "adopted" units of deployed US military service members, serving in Iraq, Afghanistan, and other conflict regions. Working within communities and through donations received from all over the country, the program assembles and ships care packages to adopted units every month until they return home. The unique program allows caring Americans to donate their time and talent to honor those serving our country during these difficult times.

Care packages can include a variety of different items. Some common items included are snacks and treats (chewing gum, lollipops, nuts, trail mix, instant coffee, hot chocolate), personal hygiene  items (toothpaste, tissues, sunscreen, batteries, puzzle books, calling cards, stationary), and seasonal items (winter holiday cards, decorations, hand and foot warmers, gloves).

The program is located in the San Francisco Bay area and is affiliated with the American Red Cross. They are currently supporting up to 200 military units on a monthly basis.

A 1st Sergeant recently wrote to express his gratitude, "I wanted to let you know that we are the very happy recipients of two more of your boxes full of food, hygiene gear and miscellaneous items."

"We are so very thankful for your support! The reminders of home we receive through the simple items you send are immeasurable. Hard to explain how deodorant or body wash makes someone happy, but it really does. I can hear it in the exclamation, like a hard-won treasure was unearthed, and I can see it when they leave as they smell the wash, flip through a magazine, or immediately sit and tear open the 'goodie' salivating before it's out of the package."

"Perhaps hard to imagine, but it is those reminders of home, those simple pleasures we miss, and favorite items that can make an entire week much more endurable. Thank you again for making our time here much more bearable."

How to Help

You can donate online or by mailing a check to the address below. 100% of all donations are used for care package items and shipping costs. Please make checks payable to ARC Operation: Care and Comfort.

You can assemble your own packages and send them to the address below. Visit Operation: Care and Comfort online for suggested items.

Contact Information

Operation: Care and Comfort
2392 Walden Square
San Jose, CA 95124
408-373-8635
troopsupport@comcast.net
Website: http://operationcareandcomfort.org.
Donations: http://operationcareandcomfort.org/occdonate/index.html

Photo credit: Operation: Care and Comfort

#71

Items to Lift Morale

GIVE 2 THE TROOPS

Summary

You can provide messages of support to service members in combat zones, as well as humanitarian items that will be distributed to Afghan people, particularly needy children.

Description

Give 2 The Troops supports the physical, moral, and spiritual health of America's Armed Forces in combat zones around the world through letters and packages prepared and shipped by caring volunteers. The organization collects donations from people around the world that are distributed to troops based on their specific requests.

These care packages help lift the morale of the troops. They also let our service members know that they have a large support system back home. Each package includes letters of support, and the items are placed into freezer bags which have positive messages written on them. These bags are often re-used by the service members, meaning they carry their positive messages from home with them.

Some service members request items to be given to the local people through Volunteer Community Relations missions. These missions not only help needy people in a foreign country, but they bring great pleasure to the troops who can share donations with individuals who are living in poverty and in terrible conditions.

After receiving several boxes of items specifically to help the local people in Afghanistan, one service member sent a letter of thanks with the following story.

"I took a bunch of donations out to the local villages to hand out. I was standing in the middle of a village that looked like it was inhabitable. Once the kids saw us, they flocked to us to see if we had anything for them. Usually we only give out a bottle of water, or a pen or pencil, or something from our MRE Kit (meals ready to eat). But this time was different. We had boxes of donations from Give2TheTroops. I noticed two little girls standing in the back of the crowd, almost hiding. I motioned to the girls to come closer, and moved the adults out of the way. I reassured them it was okay. They felt like they were walking on a cloud knowing that the American Soldiers were there and helping them. I handed each girl a bag of candy and a stuffed animal. One girl said 'Sergeant you are my friend I love you.' I now look for your boxes to see how I can give things to others."

How To Help

You can make a monetary donation online, or by mail to the donation address below.

You can donate items such as old cell phones and printer cartridges. To find a complete list of accepted items, visit the Give 2 The Troops website.

You can also volunteer your time at packing parties, by organizing donation drives, writing letters, and decorating freezer bags.

If you wish for your donation to be earmarked specifically for Afghanistan, please include a note with your donation.

Contact Information

Give2TheTroops, Inc.
196 West St,
Rocky Hill, Ct. 06067-3554

Donations:
Give2TheTroops, Inc.
P.O. Box 445
Canton, Ct. 06019-0445
888-876-6775
Andi@Give2thetroops.org
Website: www.Give2thetroops.org
Donations: www.give2thetroops.org/donations.htm

#72

Marines Afghanistan Request Fund

SPIRIT OF AMERICA

Summary

You can help US Marines by supporting their requests for goods to benefit the Afghan people. These items improve relations, save lives and support the success of the Marines' mission.

Description

At the request of Marines, and with the support of donors like you, Spirit of America has provided: farming and construction tools, solar lanterns, medical supplies, irrigation equipment, school supplies, gear and clothing for Afghan National Security Forces, sewing machines, clothing, sandals, blankets and more. All of these items benefit local Afghan people.

Here are some of the things Marines have said about Spirit of America's support.

General James Mattis, Commander, US Joint Forces Command, "Spirit of America provides direct support to our efforts to build the hopes of the people we are trying to protect from the terrorists' grip. Spirit of America's support is often as important as a resupply of ammunition as we work to turn the people against the enemy."

Lt. General Joseph Dunford, Commanding General, I Marine Expeditionary Force and Marine Corps Forces Central Command, "Our challenge in Afghanistan right now is to gain the trust, confidence and support of the Afghan people. Spirit of America is tangible evidence of the good will of the American people.

HELP THOSE WHO SERVE

It contributes to a climate of trust and confidence between our Marines and the local people. In the current fight, it's clear that actions speak louder than words ... SoA is all about action!"

LtCol David Odom, Commander, 3rd Battalion, 8th Marines, "As an infantry battalion commander tasked with conducting distributed counterinsurgency operations across a broad and contested area of operations, Spirit of America enabled me to have 'deeper-pockets' to reach into and facilitate needs and requirements for the local Afghans. The ready, willing and available support from SoA has a significant and quick impact on winning the current fight."

1st Lt. Mike Kuiper, "The people here are starting to realize that the Taliban are just hungry for power, while we are here to help them have a better life. Gifts like the ones Spirit of America provides go a long way to win in Afghanistan and get our men back safe."

This is an opportunity to directly support the safety and success of Marines in Afghanistan and to provide crucial humanitarian assistance to the Afghan people.

How to Help

You can make a donation online, by phone or by check. 100% of your contribution will be used to buy and ship the items requested by Marines to help the Afghan people.

If donating by check, make payable to Spirit of America and write "Marines/Afghanistan" in the check memo area to make sure your donation is properly allocated.

Contact Information

Spirit of America
12021 Wilshire Blvd., Suite 507
Los Angeles, CA 90025
800-819-7875
staff@spiritofamerica.net
Website: www.spiritofamerica.net
Donations: www.spiritofamerica.net/projects/172

Photo credit: SSGT William Greeson

#73

Military Pet Foster Homes

GUARDIAN ANGELS FOR SOLDIERS' PETS

Summary

You can provide a safe, temporary home for pets of service members being deployed overseas.

Description

Service members being deployed overseas must say goodbye to their family and friends, and for many that also includes their pets. Without a good home to take care of the animals, they are often forced to give them up. And with many animal shelters and rescue centers being overcrowded, it can mean a Soldier's beloved pet must be put down.

Guardian Angels for Soldiers' Pets (GASP) foster home program is designed to provide an alternative to the unwanted surrender of beloved pets of deploying military service members. The organization does this by recruiting and qualifying volunteer foster homes who are willing to open their homes to provide a loving and safe environment for these pets until they can be reunited upon their owners' return. Beyond preparing for veterinary care and basic food/supply needs, this service is provided at no cost to the military service member.

When a foster home needed request is made, GASP works with the military service member to match their pet(s) with an appropriate foster home. It facilitates the foster home placement using the Foster Home Agreement - a written agreement that outlines the terms of the relationship and protects the interests of all parties involved.

GASP's affiliated Chapters and state specific Volunteer Directors/Foster Home Coordinators provide further assistance by attending pet introduction visits, placement visit, and homecoming meeting. During the foster term, where resources are available all efforts are made to remain in contact with the foster home to ensure the pet remains in a loving and safe environment, plus work with

HELP THOSE WHO SERVE

foster home caregivers in regards to any issues or concerns that may arise.

Where resources permit, short term foster (up to 9 months) is also available for pets of active military, military family with a deployed spouse, and veterans experiencing a qualifying emergency hardship. Currently these type of foster home requests are handled on a case-by-case basis.

How To Help

You can make a donation online or by check.

You can become a foster home for military pets. Visit the GASP website for more information on applying.

Contact Information

Guardian Angels for Soldiers' Pets
167 Candleberry Circle
Hot Springs, AR 71913-2019
501-325-1591
info@guardianangelsforsoldierspet.org
Website: www.guardianangelsforsoldierspet.org
Donations: www.guardianangelsforsoldierspet.org

#74

Mobile Counseling and Services for Vets

HOPE4HEROES

Summary

You can provide veterans who are transitioning from military to civilian life with mobile counseling that will come to them.

Description

Hope4Heroes was founded by veterans to support veterans and families in a variety of areas. It provides much-needed services for veterans and service members transitioning from military to civilian life.

Hope4Heroes is currently developing its newest initiative, the Mobile Veterans Support Center (MVSC). Teams of mobile "coaches" (counselors, case managers, and health educators) will travel to cities and towns across the nation to provide greater reach and better access for veterans. The services offered will include crisis counseling and job transition training.

The coaches will travel in a customized truck and trailer that will serve as a fully-operational office. There will be a waiting room, private rooms for counseling, work stations, computers, and Wi-Fi access. Literature, counseling, and workshops will be made available with the help of local volunteers at each location.

Hope4Heroes offers many other programs that aim to make the transition from military to civilian life easier. Soldiers returning from Iraq and Afghanistan who are in need of financial assistance or education grants for their children can receive assistance. Career transition training and resume writing courses help service members looking for civilian jobs. Hope4Heroes also offers counseling to service members suffering from PTSD and TBI.

HELP THOSE WHO SERVE

"We all owe a debt of gratitude to those who serve. It is rewarding to be able to help the heroes that have sacrificed and suffered to protect myself and my children," said Hope4Heroes founder Vic Luebker. "Hope4Heroes is our way of thanking and honoring the memories of the brave men and women who fought for our freedom, protected us when we could not protect ourselves, and gave us hope for a better future when we thought all hope was lost."

How To Help

You can make a donation online. To earmark donations specifically for Afghanistan, email Hope4Heroes directly.

You can volunteer to help with fundraising events or to become part of the service-oriented volunteer force. Visit the Hope4Heroes website to see what opportunities are available.

You can thank a hero. Messages submitted on the Hope4Heroes website are mailed to the organization Any Soldier, and then distributed to service members.

Contact Information

Hope4Heroes
c/o Vic Luebker
12274 Bandera Rd., #236
San Antonio, TX 78023
210-544.8319
info@hope4heroes.org
Website: www.hope4heroes.org
Donations: www.hope4heroes.org/donations
Thank a Hero: www.hope4heroes.org/thank-a-hero

#75

Nature Retreats for Veterans

WOUNDED WARRIOR PROJECT

Summary

You can help wounded warriors suffering from combat stress receive rehabilitation and peer support during nature retreats.

Description

The Wounded Warrior Project believes in the power of nature and recreation to help warriors dealing with combat stress. Project Odyssey, an outdoor rehabilitative retreat that combines adventure challenges with opportunities for peer support and group processing, was created to support warriors in their recovery from combat stress.

Recreational experiences ranging from rock climbing in the Black Hills of South Dakota to herding cattle on Wildcatter Ranch, encourage personal growth among participants and team building within the warrior community.

In conjunction with the National Park Service, Project Odyssey takes place on a variety of geographical locations over the course of five days. Past event sites include Wildcatter Resort & Ranch in Graham, Texas; Marriott Cocoa Beach in Miami, Florida; National Ability Center, Park City, Utah; Acadia National Park in Maine. Each location offers a unique experience that is different from the last and varies based on geographical resources.

Partnering with the Vet Centers across the country, Wounded Warrior Project recruits combat warriors from across the country who are currently enrolled in counseling services. Odyssey allows participants to continue their therapeutic journey in a novel, dynamic setting with peers and support from Wounded Warrior Project and Vet Center professionals.

Participant Requirements:

- Currently seeking treatment for combat stress

- Has never been on Project Odyssey
- Can travel independently to the Project Odyssey location
- Has been screened by a licensed clinician

A Project Odyssey participant, Wildcatter Ranch 2008, wrote, "My recovery from combat stress is a continuous journey that began in Iraq and continues on the homefront."

How To Help

You can make a donation online or by mail. Checks should be accompanied by a donation form that can be found on the WWP website.

You can donate through the Combined Federal Campaign, CFC #11425.

Contact Information

Wounded Warrior Project
P.O. Box 758517
Topeka, KS 66675-8517
877-832-6997
info@woundedwarriorproject.org
Website: www.woundedwarriorproject.org
Donations: www.woundedwarriorproject.org

#76

Online Directory of Service Members' Needs

USA TOGETHER

Summary

You can directly connect with an injured service member and help fulfill their needs as they recover.

Description

USA Together brings together injured service members who need assistance with people who want to help. The organization posts requests from injured Soldiers and their families for goods (baby cribs, laptops for jobs), services (bathroom modification for wheelchair access, legal help), or modest financial assistance. An email notification then goes out to those who have signed up to help.

Founder and Executive Director of USA Together, Dave Mahler, describes the site as "a Craigslist for wounded warriors."

The site takes requests from any current or former military service members, including National Guard, Reserves and Coast Guard, who have service connected injuries. Families of the fallen also qualify to post requests.

The request posts include the background of the Soldier asking for help, the branch of the armed forces they served in, where they currently live, what they are asking for, and how much it will cost to provide. Many also include photos of themselves and their families.

Anyone wishing to help can visit the site to read about current requests and learn more about the individuals or families they are helping. The personal connection between those who donate and the injured Soldiers is a driving force of the project.

HELP THOSE WHO SERVE

The Chicago Tribune provided a great example of USA Together's efforts in a 2009 article,* "For Army Sgt. Leonard "Leo" Kaalberg, the help could not come soon enough. A roadside bomb in Iraq in July 2007 left the burly former high school defensive end with pounding headaches, short-term memory loss and severe nerve damage on the left side of his body. Today, the 28-year-old Moline father of four, the recipient of two Purple Hearts, is struggling to reinvent himself while humbled by the most basic of tasks. On some days, Kaalberg's left side hurts so much that he can't pick up his infant son.

Kaalberg's request? Clothes for his children: ages 7, 5, 3 and 9 months.

Response was swift. One recent evening, the organization posted the request for $500 worth of clothing and diapers. The profile included a photo, a brief note about Kaalberg and a list of his children's clothing sizes. By 12:30 p.m. the next day, 14 people had responded from across the country. Several reached out even after his $500 request had been met, asking how else they might assist the retired Soldier.

Kaalberg said he was floored by the reaction. He stumbled a bit over his words when asked to describe how the outpouring felt. "It's really hard to ... how do you say 'thank you' to people you've never met? It surprised me so much."

*Reprinted with permission of *The Chicago Tribune*.

How To Help

You can make a donation online or by check. Donations can be made to fill a specific request financially or through an item or service donation.

Volunteers are encouraged to check the website to see what help is currently needed across the country.

Contact Information

USAtogether, Inc
171 Main Street, #106
Los Altos, CA 94022
Info@USAtogether.org
Website: www.USAtogether.org
Donations: www.USAtogether.org

#77

Peer Mentoring for Veterans

WOUNDED WARRIOR PROJECT

Summary

You can help provide peer-to-peer and benefits counseling to returning wounded veterans.

Description

During a wounded warrior's initial recovery, often the most positive influence is the friendship and understanding of a peer mentor, a fellow wounded warrior. It is critically important for the newly injured to know someone who has traveled before them on the same rocky road. Wounded Warrior Project (WWP) staff and alumni are excellent resources, listeners and "hospital buddies" who can share their understanding and perspective from their own real-life successes.

The organization's peer mentors are also available to visit with the wounded warrior's family, if requested. Peer mentors can help family members visualize the achievements possible through rehabilitation and hard work.

In addition to the peer mentoring program, WWP provides and fosters opportunities for informal peer interaction, where WWP Alumni can meet, support, and inspire newly injured warriors.

Benefits counselors also work with severely wounded service members as soon as they return to the United States. Counselors provide guidance and help to navigate government benefits available to military personnel and their families. They also help build connections between wounded warriors, establishing a network of peers to provide the necessary assistance, friendship, and inspiration.

How To Help

You can make a donation online or by mail. Checks should be accompanied by a donation form that can be found on the WWP website.

HELP THOSE WHO SERVE

You can donate through the Combined Federal Campaign, CFC #11425.

Contact Information

Wounded Warrior Project
P.O. Box 758517
Topeka, KS 66675-8517
877-832-6997
info@woundedwarriorproject.org
Website: www.woundedwarriorproject.org
Donations: www.woundedwarriorproject.org

#78

Rehabilitative Cycling Event for Wounded Warriors

WOUNDED WARRIOR PROJECT

Summary

You can sponsor a wounded warrior as they ride in a rehabilitative event aimed at raising awareness and their self-confidence.

Description

The Soldier Ride, at its core, is a rehabilitative cycling event designed to challenge our wounded warriors to get back in the saddle, both literally and figuratively. It also is a tool to help both the physical and mental wounds of war. These rides also raise awareness for the Wounded Warrior Project (WWP) mission and its many important programs designed to serve our injured and their families, and in turn raise money through sponsorships, pledges and donations.

Even though the service members have already given so much, they want to give this positive message to the public and pass the message on to the next group of wounded Soldiers.

Many of these men and women who participate have been physically active throughout their lives and do not want to lose that. They get on the bikes to prove to themselves that they can still do it. Soldier Ride is not about politics, it's not about the war, it's simply about the Soldiers.

The wounded veterans are the embodiment of the spirit of this country and they make us all proud to say we are Americans.

Here is what some participants have said about the ride:

"I can't say how great the Soldier Ride was. Because of your association, I was able to meet many others who have been through similar and oh so traumatic events greater than myself. It has been my honor to have the privilege to ride along with true heroes and friends. Where WWP is now is a tribute to the men

HELP THOSE WHO SERVE

and women who make it up. I am a stronger person today thanks to WWP."

"I wanted to thank you for the opportunity once again to participate in Soldier Ride. I had an epiphany today while I was riding. I thought back to the days where I hated my life and felt utterly useless. Then I agreed to go on my first Soldier Ride. WOW!!!! The feeling of empowerment. I believe I've come full circle in what Soldier Ride has to offer. I can honestly say it saved me. It gave me a physical and mental outlet which is cycling. You gave me that. All of you did. I'm eternally grateful."

How To Help

You can make a donation online or by mail. Checks should be accompanied by a donation form that can be found on the WWP website.

You can donate through the Combined Federal Campaign, CFC #11425.

If your business is interested in sponsoring a wounded warrior, please contact WWP directly.

Contact Information

Wounded Warrior Project
P.O. Box 758517
Topeka, KS 66675-8517
877-832-6997
info@woundedwarriorproject.org
Website: http://sr.woundedwarriorproject.org
Donations: www.woundedwarriorproject.org

#79

Saying "Thank You"

Summary

Show your appreciation by personally thanking a Soldier, Sailor, Airman or Marine for his or her service.

Description

America's Soldiers, Sailors, Airmen and Marines serve and sacrifice for us all. Much of the time they serve far from home and under difficult and dangerous conditions. It makes a difference to them to know that they are remembered and appreciated. As General David Petraeus, Commander, United States Central Command, says, ""Nothing means more to those in harm's way than the knowledge that their country appreciates their sacrifices and those of their families."

Sergeant Rock Conley tells how important this is to those who serve, "I would just like to tell America, thank you for all of your support and love you give us… it keeps our heads up and lets us know just who we are fighting for – all of YOU. It's no wonder why I'd give the ultimate sacrifice to keep our great country free and safe. Every time I come back, I get applause, handshakes, smiles, cheers, pats on the back, and thank yous. It makes me feel good, knowing that I am doing my part protecting this great country. Thank you and God Bless."

How To Help

Take the opportunity to thank our military personnel in person when the chance arises. A simple "Thank you for your service" or "I appreciate your service to our country" will be welcome. Add a smile and handshake, if you can.

When a group of service members from your area is returning home, it is the perfect chance to show your support. Look to your local paper or radio station to find out where they will be coming in. Gather your family and friends and greet them with cheers and smiles.

HELP THOSE WHO SERVE

If you feel uncomfortable approaching a service member, you can still say thanks with a silent gesture. The Gratitude Campaign has created a way to tell someone "Thank you from the bottom of my heart" without saying a word.

Adapted from American Sign Language, the sign allows you to communicate quickly and easily. Place your right hand on your heart as though you are saying the Pledge of Allegiance. Then slowly lower your hand, down and out, bending at the elbow. Stop for a moment at about your belly button, with your hand flat, palm up, angled toward the person you're thanking.

#80

Scholarships for Military Families

PAT TILLMAN FOUNDATION –

TILLMAN MILITARY SCHOLARS PROGRAM

Summary

You can help provide educational scholarships to service members and their families. All veterans, active service members and their dependents (spouse and children) from the Armed Forces are eligible to apply.

Description

Our nation was built on the sacrifices made by the young men and women in the military who demonstrate the very kind of leadership that the Pat Tillman Foundation seeks to inspire in all young people. Yet, even with the GI Bill, many service members and their dependents (children and spouses) still lack the financial means to pursue their greater educational goals.

The Pat Tillman Foundation was established to carry forward Pat's legacy of leadership and civic action by supporting future generations of leaders who embody the American tradition of citizen service.

In 2009, the Pat Tillman Foundation awarded 52 members of the inaugural class of Tillman Military Scholars $642,000 in scholarships. The organization strives to grow the amount of funds given each year to $3.6 million, the NFL contract amount Pat walked away from when he joined the US Army.

In the aftermath of the attacks on September 11, 2001, Pat Tillman proudly put his NFL career with the Arizona Cardinals on hold to serve his country. This decision was just one of many he made over the course of his lifetime to help others and serve a cause greater than self-interest.

The Tillman family and friends created the Pat Tillman Foundation in 2004, following Pat's death while serving with the 75th Ranger Regiment in Afghanistan.

Marie Tillman, co-founder of Pat Tillman Foundation and wife of Pat Tillman states, "We can think of no better way to celebrate Pat's life and legacy than providing the support necessary for our veterans and their families to achieve their academic dreams."

How to Help

You can make a donation online, by mail or by fax.

You can volunteer for or participate in Pat's Run, the foundation's annual fundraising event at Sun Devil Stadium.

You can purchase and wear Pat Tillman jerseys and exclusive Pat's Run gear. Proceeds benefit the Pat Tillman Foundation.

For additional ways to donate, such as tribute gifts, workplace campaigns, and planned giving, visit the website.

Contact Information

Pat Tillman Foundation
2121 South Mill Avenue, Suite 214
Tempe, Arizona 85282
480-621-4074
info@pattillmanfoundation.org
Website: www.pattillmanfoundation.org
Donations: http://pattillmanfoundation.org/donate.aspx

#81

Send Thanks to Soldiers

A MILLION THANKS

Summary

You can thank those who serve in many creative and personal ways that will boost spirits and morale.

Description

A Million Thanks is a year-round campaign to show our appreciation to our US Military Men and Women, past and present for their sacrifices, dedication, and service to our country through our letters, emails, cards, and prayers.

A Million Thanks asks individuals, schools, churches, and businesses around the US to participate by having their students, congregations, and customers write letters, cards, email messages, or prayer messages. The organization then forwards the message to a service man or women, either active duty or retired, through its many contacts. Your messages will also be delivered to many USOs and Veterans Hospitals for distribution.

There are some basic rules that must be followed:

- All letters and/or cards will be screened for security reasons
- If you are sending more than one letter or card, do not place in individual envelopes
- Handmade cards are preferred
- Any size card will be accepted
- Do not use glitter on cards
- Candy or other food items cannot be accepted and should not be included or attached to cards
- Military personnel love to communicate with us - you can include your name, address or email address if you so desire
- Photos of your family, church, or classroom participants can add a personal touch to your card, but must be appropriate

The more positive the message the better - care should be taken not to refer to anything that may cause grief or uneasiness to the military reader who may be serving

If you are mailing letters/cards in bulk (100 or more from a school, company or organization), bundle them in units of 100 using two rubber bands wrapped one lengthwise and the other widthwise. This aids the organization in sorting.

How to Help

You can make a donation online or by check.

You can make cards and write letters to send to our service members and veterans. Visit the A Million Thanks website for guidelines and to find your nearest drop-off location. Cards and letters may also be mailed in.

Contact Information

A Million Thanks
17853 Santiago Blvd., #107-355
Villa Park, CA 92861
AMillionThanks@aol.com
Website: www.amillionthanks.org
Donations: www.amillionthanks.org/Donation.asp

#82

Soldiers Afghanistan Request Fund

SPIRIT OF AMERICA

Summary

You can help American Soldiers by supporting their requests for goods to benefit the Afghan people. These items improve relations, save lives and support the success of the Soldiers' mission.

Description

At the request of Soldiers, and with the support of donors like you, Spirit of America has provided: medical equipment and supplies, saffron bulbs and farming tools, water purification equipment, clothing, school supplies, toys, blankets, shoes and more. All of these items benefit local Afghan people.

Here are some of the things American Soldiers say about the value of Spirit of America's support.

Sgt. Major Mack McDowell, "The Taliban's biggest ally is that the local people are destitute, and hungry for any good deed. Thank you so much for enabling us. We are truly thankful for the ability to make a positive influence on those who need it the most. Words can't express how much your efforts mean to us."

Chaplain Brian Murphy, "Spirit of America's things save lives here. When you help a family, when you show people that you care, they refuse to be used by the terrorist. When you help us to help them, you serve right along side of us.

HELP THOSE WHO SERVE

The compassion of the American Soldier is one of the most powerful weapons in our arsenal."

Major Eric Ruthman, "Afghan adults, parents, friends and family of these children see us helping them which enhances feelings of good will toward US and Coalition."

This is an opportunity to directly support the safety and success of Soldiers in Afghanistan, and to provide humanitarian assistance to the Afghan people.

How to Help

You can make a donation online, by phone or by check. 100% of your contribution will be used to buy and ship the items requested by American Soldiers to help the Afghan people.

If donating by check, make payable to Spirit of America and write "Soldiers/ Afghanistan" in the check memo area to make sure your donation is properly allocated.

Contact Information

Spirit of America
12021 Wilshire Blvd., Suite 507
Los Angeles, CA 90025
800-819-7875
staff@spiritofamerica.net
Website: www.spiritofamerica.net
Donations: www.spiritofamerica.net/projects/71

Photo credits: Scott Koeman, Rachel Hudak

#83

Steak Dinners for Wounded at Walter Reed

THE ALEETHIA FOUNDATION

Summary

You can lift spirits and provide a Friday night steak dinner to injured patients at the Walter Reed Army Medical Center and the National Naval Medical Center.

Description

Seriously injured service members recovering at Walter Reed Army Medical Center and National Naval Medical Centers have the opportunity to gather with their families and other recovering patients to enjoy a weekly steak dinner. The benefits of the dinners are abundant. They provide a social environment for these disabled and often isolated service members, many of whom are unable to leave their hospital rooms during the week.

The Aleethia Foundation started Friday Night Steak Dinners as a night out for two Soldiers in 2003, but has since grown into a commitment to honor and support the newly injured service members and their families during their recovery process. The dinner provides much more than a warm meal for the

patients. It also is an integral part of their healing process as they are provided the opportunity to share their stories, talk about their injuries, and discuss what has helped them the most during their recovery process.

Invitations are given to patients in the medical centers and those in other residential facilities on the hospital grounds, as well as their families, volunteers and medical personnel. The dinners are held in a variety of places, such as restaurants, private clubs, ambassador residences, baseball stadium, and private country clubs. But in each location, dinner is served in a private area where patients can feel at home with their fellow service members.

In the first six years, The Aleethia Foundation has been able to provide more than 22,000 dinners for injured service members and their families. But it is the service members themselves who have experienced Friday Night Steak Dinners who can best explain its benefits.

Staff Sergeant Metzdorf, "I've never seen Soldiers helping Soldiers like that – ever. It was the most positive experience you could have during a week of recovery. It was just awesome."

Staff Sergeant Calhoun, "I can remember waiting all week for the dinners. It was good atmosphere for us to get out of the hospital, eat well and think of what the future holds."

Staff Sergeant Clements, "Friday night dinners helped me to realize that I wasn't alone in my battle and recovery."

Sergeant Clark, "My first dinner was the first time I felt like I was home."

How To Help

You can make a donation of any size online or by a check. Individuals and organizations can also sponsor a Friday night dinner by emailing the organization.

Contact Information

The Aleethia Foundation
Hal Koster, Founder/Executive Director
1718 M Street NW, Suite 1170
Washington, DC 20036
202-714-0135
hal@aleethia.org
Website: www.aleethia.org
Donations: www.aleethia.org/support/index.php

Photo credit: The Aleethia Foundation

#84

Support for Schools with Military Children

DONORSCHOOSE.ORG

Summary

You can support classroom projects that benefit public school students with parents in the military. This supports innovative learning projects for service members' children.

Description

DonorsChoose.org is a website where people from all walks of life can make a tangible difference in public schools. While family members serve our country abroad, you can support their children here at home.

Teachers post requests on the website for materials and experiences that their students need to thrive. Project requests range from paper and pencils to field trips and science kits. The idea is to unleash the creativity of frontline teachers who are too often constrained by a lack of funding.

You can make a donation to the project request that most inspires you. DonorsChoose. org then delivers the materials to the school, and sends you photos and thank-you letters from the classroom you chose to help, along with an itemized cost report showing how each dollar was spent.

At DonorsChoose.org, someone giving $5 gets the same choice, transparency, and vivid feedback that has traditionally been reserved for millionaire benefactors. The organization calls this approach "citizen philanthropy."

HELP THOSE WHO SERVE

In the spring of 2009, DonorsChoose.org's platform enabled members, veterans, and supporters of the Army, Air Force, Coast Guard, Marines, and Navy to compete for which branch could be the most generous in funding projects at schools that serve students with parents in the military. Currently, an online registry of classroom projects at DonorsChoose.org/troops-kids features requests from public school teachers serving children of military families.

Since launching in 2000, more than 110,000 teachers in public schools have posted project requests on DonorsChoose.org. Even more citizen philanthropists have responded, delivering books, art supplies, technology, and other resources to students at high-need public schools. To date, DonorsChoose.org has channeled more than $40 million worth of learning resources to more than 2.6 million students. National media, such as Oprah Winfrey and *The New York Times*, have profiled DonorsChoose.org as "the future of philanthropy."

How To Help

You can make a donation of any amount online to help fund a classroom request that speaks to you. When that project gets fully funded, you'll hear back from the teacher and students and then see your impact on the classroom you chose to support. Requests are only from public and public charter schools in the US.

You can contribute directly to a project for children of service members by visiting DonorsChoose.org/troops-kids.

Contact Information

DonorsChoose.org
347 West 36th Street
Suite 503
New York, NY 10018
Website: www.DonorsChoose.org
Donations: www.DonorsChoose.org/troops-kids

#85

Support for the Injured at Landstuhl Hospital

LANDSTUHL HOSPITAL CARE PROJECT

Summary

You can provide injured service members recovering in the Landstuhl Hospital in Germany with items of comfort and relief.

Description

The mission of Landstuhl Hospital Care Project (LHCP) is to help support the Pastoral Services Department at Landstuhl Regional Medical Center (LRMC) in Germany and field hospitals in combat areas. LHCP provides comfort and relief items for military members who become sick, injured or wounded from service in Iraq, Kuwait, and Afghanistan. Donated items are distributed to military patients at Landstuhl Regional Medical Center, or are sent to field hospitals with needs that we have learned about from patient liaisons. LHCP currently supports Operation Enduring Freedom (OEF) and Operation Iraqi Freedom (OIF).

Many of the military personnel are grievously wounded and require long hospitalization and rehabilitation. The purpose of LHCP's program is to enhance the morale and welfare of the wounded by contributing quality of life items such as sweat pants, sweat shirts, pajamas, lounge pants, boxers, socks, and seasonal jackets or coats. Combat Support Hospitals also receive items such as sheets, blankets, pillows, and towels. Each shipment that Landstuhl Hospital Care Project sends is sent in honor of a military member who has made the ultimate sacrifice and lost his or her life in service to our country.

LHCP was founded to provide sweat suits for our wounded military to wear as they received care at LRMC. As the group grew, the mission expanded. The organization's major goal now is to get the Chaplains the items they require to provide support and comfort for our men and woman to convalesce. The needs change month to month, and so do the goals of the LHCP.

The funds raised are used to purchase needed items, and the items that are donated from LHCP lists fill LRMC and field hospital requests. Your donations will help our Soldiers, Sailors, Airmen, and Marines know that they are supported.

How To Help

You can make a donation online or by check.

You can donate needed items. For a list of items in need, visit the LHCP website.

Contact Information

Landstuhl Hospital Care Project
Sharon Buck, LHCP Treasurer
52 Seminole Trail
Ft. Mitchell, AL 36856

Send Needed Items to:
Landstuhl Hospital Care Project
29 Greenleaf Terrace
Stafford, Virginia 22556
LHCP.President@yahoo.com
Website: www.landstuhlhospitalcareproject.org
Donations: www.landstuhlhospitalcareproject.org

#86

Therapy Dogs for Injured Service Members

PENNY'S FROM HEAVEN FOUNDATION

Summary

You can help injured service members recover with the assistance of a specially-trained therapy dog.

Description

Penny's From Heaven Foundation is an elite group of well-trained, exceptional-working therapy dogs. The therapy dogs provide services to returning wounded servicemen and women, long-term care facilities, and rehabilitation hospitals. The therapy dogs are also present at service members' deployments and Yellow Ribbon ceremonies.

The dogs meet an extreme need in any and all situations, dealing with burn survivors, amputees, and Soldiers with visible and invisible wounds such as Post Traumatic Stress Disorder (PTSD) and Traumatic Brain Injuries (TBI).

Penny's From Heaven Foundation therapy dogs are trained to assist with depression, fine and gross motor coordination, trunk and shoulder stability, motivation, confidence, balance, speech, memory skills, problem solving, distraction from pain, walking difficulties, identification of naming objects, following directions, attention to task and much more.

The organization has a special group of working therapy dogs that provide one-on-one therapeutic intervention and Solution Focused Therapeutic intervention (SFT) in rehabilitation settings. These dogs are used as a modality to reach a specific goal or expectation with a patient. These therapy dogs and situations are under the guidance of healthcare professionals (occupational therapists, physical therapists, speech therapists and neuropsychologists) and the handlers have about a 99% success rate. The results become part of the

HELP THOSE WHO SERVE

patient's medical records.

Another elite group of therapy dogs are PTSD Support Dogs, affording comfort and support to the returning wounded Soldiers with PTSD and TBI. These working therapy dogs are selected and trained for this specific purpose. Through recognition, education, acceptance, treatment and support, Penny's From Heaven Foundation is promoting the use and benefits of trained working therapy dogs with PTSD patients.

How To Help

You can make a donation online or by check.

Contact Information

Penny's From Heaven Foundation, Inc.
1915 Eagle Meadow
San Antonio, TX 78248
210-493-5101
Patsy@pennysfromheavenfoundation.org
Website: www.pennysfromheavenfoundation.org
Donations: www.pennysfromheavenfoundation.org

#87

Transition Teams for Injured Service Members

AMERICAN LEGION – HEROES TO HOMETOWNS

Summary

You can ease the transition of severely injured service members, and their families, from active duty to civilian life.

Description

The Heroes to Hometowns program is a transition-assistance program for US service members who have been severely injured in the global war on terrorism. Severely injured refers to service members who suffered blindness, total hearing loss, an amputation, severe body burns, traumatic brain injury or a spinal-cord injury.

Heroes to Hometowns can provide:

- A Welcome-home celebration
- Temporary Financial Assistance
- Pro-bono financial planning
- Housing assistance
- Home and vehicle adaptation
- Government claims assistance
- Entertainment options
- Family support

You can help by forming a Hero Transition Team for a returning service member. A Hero Transition Team is a community-based support team to rally and coordinate assistance for a service member leaving the military and entering civilian life.

You do not have to be a veteran to conduct a Heroes to Hometown program. The American Legion is willing to work with anyone for the benefit of severely

HELP THOSE WHO SERVE

injured service members.

The National Guard is a national partner in the Heroes to Hometowns program. As such, the National Guard has provided its Web-based resources to aid in the outreach to military members and their families.

How to Help

You can make a monetary donation online.

Form a Transition Team in your community. You can request assistance and promotional materials for your program by visiting the American Legion web site.

Contact Information

The American Legion
Heroes To Hometowns
202-631-9924
heroestohometowns@legion.org
Website: www.legion.org
Donations: www.legion.org/donations
Team Formation Assistance: www.legion.org/heroes/assistance
Promotional Materials: www.legion.org/heroes/materials

#88

Travel Help for Military Families

LUKE'S WINGS

Summary

You can help a family travel to see their injured service member by providing travel arrangements and tickets.

Description

Luke's Wings is an organization dedicated to the support of service members who have been wounded in battle. Recognizing the immediate need for families to be with their loved ones at such a difficult time, Luke's Wings provides families with the means to visit during the service member's hospitalization and rehabilitation.

The organization purchases travel agency services and travel tickets for the service member's family. With the support of loved ones at their side, the service members receive the encouragement and motivation they need during their recovery.

Recognizing the difficulties families encounter as they make their way to their loved ones' side, Luke's Wings partners with corporations whenever possible to ease the burden on families and service members during their visit. Luke's Wings looks to its corporate partners to help provide free  or discounted pricing for things such as hotel accommodations, entertainment, meals and local travel vouchers.

Service members can face months and even years of in-hospital recovery. That was the situation with Adam, an Army Corporal injured during his service in Afghanistan.

Adam was severely wounded during an ambush by an RPG, an IED, and a bullet that shattered the bone in his left leg. He was flown back to Walter Reed where he spent 22 months undergoing surgeries and blood transfusions. His parents took turns flying across the country to see him whenever they could. The cost of traveling and missing work, as well as increased airline prices, took its toll and soon they were unable to afford any more trips.

Adam wrote to Luke's Wings to request that his mother and father be flown to visit him for his father's birthday. His wish was granted and they were finally able to spend a few days together as a family. His mother wrote to Luke's Wings to express her gratitude:

"As the holidays come to an end I wanted to tell you Thank you so much for your wonderful gift. My husband and I flew to Upper state New York to see Adam for his father's birthday. It was a dream come true. We saw Adam, who by the way is getting stronger every day, we also saw our grandchild Tucker for the first time. Our time together was wonderful. We participated in putting up Adam, Stephanie, and Tucker's first real Christmas tree. We had a birthday dinner for Big Rick in the small town of Mexico, New York. Best of all we spent 5 wonderful days as a family."

"We are very proud of Adam and his service to our country. We are very blessed that after 22 months his wounds are healing and he will close out his Army career. But, because of your caring organization we spent 5 magical days with our Soldier. Words will never convey how thankful we are."

How to Help

You can make a monetary donation online or by mail.

Contact Information

Luke's Wings
20 Ritchfield Court
Rockville, MD 20850
information@lukeswings.org
Website: www.lukeswings.org
Donate: www.lukeswings.org/donate.htm

Photo credit: Luke's Wings

#89

Treatment and Research for Traumatic Brain Injury

INTREPID FALLEN HEROES FUND

Summary

You can help military personnel suffering from traumatic brain injury by supporting the construction of the National Intrepid Center of Excellence.

Description

The Intrepid Fallen Heroes Fund has provided more than $65 million in support for the families of military personnel lost in service to our nation, and for severely wounded military personnel and veterans. These efforts are funded entirely with donations from the public, and hundreds of thousands of individuals have contributed to the Fund. 100% of contributions raised by the Intrepid Fallen Heroes Fund go towards these programs; all administrative expenses are underwritten by the Fund's Trustees.

From 2000 to 2005, the Fund provided close to $20 million to families of United States military personnel lost in performance of their duty, mostly in service in Iraq and Afghanistan. The Fund provided unrestricted grants of $11,000 to each spouse and $5,000 to each dependent child; and $1,000 to parents of unmarried service members. The payments were coordinated with the casualty offices of the Armed Forces, to ensure all families received these benefits. In 2005, a new law substantially increased the benefits granted to these families, and the Fund redirected its support toward the severely injured.

In January 2007, the Fund completed construction of a $45 million, state-of-the-art physical rehabilitation center at Brooke Army Medical Center in San Antonio, Texas. The "Center for the Intrepid" serves military personnel who have been catastrophically disabled in operations in Iraq and Afghanistan, and veterans severely injured in other operations and in the normal performance of their duties. The 60,000 square-foot Center provides space and facilities for the rehabilitation needs of the patients and their caregivers. The Center is co-located with two 21-room Fisher Houses that house the families of patients.

The current project, The National Intrepid Center of Excellence (NICoE), will be an advanced facility dedicated to research, diagnosis and treatment of military personnel and veterans suffering from traumatic brain injury (TBI) and psychological health issues. NICoE will be a 72,000 square foot, two-story facility located on the Navy campus at Bethesda, Maryland, adjacent to the new Walter Reed National Military Medical Center, with close access to the Uniformed Services University, the National Institutes of Health, and the Veterans Health Administration. NICoE will be designed to provide the most advanced services for advanced diagnostics, initial treatment plan and family education, introduction to therapeutic modalities, referral and reintegration support for military personnel and veterans with TBI, post traumatic stress disorder, and/or complex psychological health issues. Further, NICoE will conduct research, test new protocols and provide comprehensive training and education to patients, providers and families while maintaining ongoing telehealth follow-up care across the country and throughout the world.

How To Help

You can donate online, by phone, or by check. Mail all checks ATTN: CONTRIBUTIONS to the address below. 100% of all contributions go directly to IFHF programs.

Contact Information

Intrepid Fallen Heroes Fund
One Intrepid Square
W 46th Street & 12th Avenue
New York, NY 10036
800-340-HERO
info@fallenheroesfund.org
Website: www.fallenheroesfund.org
Donations: www.fallenheroesfund.org/donate.aspx

#90

Veteran Benefits Assistance

DISABLED AMERICAN VETERANS

Summary

You can help veterans, their dependents and survivors receive free counseling to properly file claims for assistance for programs such as disability compensation, vocational rehabilitation, and home loans.

Description

For 90 years, Disabled American Veterans (DAV) has never wavered in its commitment to serve our nation's service-connected disabled veterans, their dependents and survivors. Disabled American Veterans is a non-profit organization founded in 1020 and chartered by the US Congress in 1932. It is dedicated to one, single purpose: building better lives for our nation's 2.3 million disabled veterans and their families.

DAV employs trained National Service Officers (NSOs) to assist veterans and their families in filing claims for VA disability compensation and pension; vocational rehabilitation and employment; education; home loan guaranty; life insurance; death benefits; health care and much more. They provide free services, such as information seminars, counseling and community outreach. NSOs also represent veterans and active duty military personnel, including those wounded and injured in Afghanistan

and Iraq, before Discharge Review Boards, Boards for Correction of Military Records, Physical Evaluation Boards and other official panels.

DAV has 88 offices throughout the US and in Puerto Rico where the corps of approximately 260 NSOs represent veterans and their families with claims

HELP THOSE WHO SERVE

for benefits from the Department of Veterans Affairs (VA), the Department of Defense and other government agencies. Veterans need not be DAV members to take advantage of this outstanding assistance, which is provided free of charge to all.

In 2008, DAV represented nearly a quarter of a million veterans and their families in claims for VA benefits, obtaining for them nearly $3.4 billion in new and retroactive benefits.

DAV receives no money or grants from the federal government. The service programs are sustained by contributions from the public. DAV meets all standards and is approved by the leading consumer agency, the Better Business Bureau Wise Giving Alliance.

DAV volunteers at VA medical centers perform a wide range of duties. The role as a volunteer at a VA medical facility can be as basic, and as important, as just being a friend to a patient in the trying days of illness and therapy. In 2008, DAV volunteers contributed 464,155 hours of service to veterans at VA hospitals, clinics and nursing homes through the VA Voluntary Service program.

How To Help

You can make a monetary donation online or by phone.

You can make a $5 donation by texting "DAV" to 90999. The donation will be added to your next mobile phone bill

You can volunteer your time in a number of ways. Visit the DAV website to learn more.

Contact Information

Disabled American Veterans
PO Box 14301
Cincinnati, OH 45250-0301
877-426-2838
Website: www.dav.org
Donations: www.dav.org/donations
Volunteers: www.dav.org/volunteers

Photo credit: Disabled American Veterans

#91

Warrior Legacy Ranch

WARRIOR LEGACY FOUNDATION

Summary

You can provide mental, physical and emotional rehabilitation to Soldiers and their families through the creation of a ranch retreat.

Description

The Warrior Legacy Foundation (WLF), in conjunction with former Navy SEAL Marcus Luttrell, is creating a retreat/camp for returned Warriors and their families: The Marcus Luttrell Warrior Legacy Ranch. The ranch is designed for the express purpose of providing mental, physical and emotional rehabilitation for Soldiers returning from active duty in the US Military.

The site is slated to be 205 acres abundant in wildlife ranging from whitetail/axis deer and fish to wild turkey. The proposed ranch location is adjacent to the Frio River, a crystal clear river that runs for more than 200 miles. The design of the project consists of 25 fully-furnished 2-bedroom, 2-bathroom cabins. All cabins will be equipped for special-needs guests. In addition, there will be a 2500 sq. ft. building accommodating a fully stocked grocery store, office, game room, gym and commercial BBQ pit. The retreat would be capable of housing up to 75 guests at any one time.

The retreat will have many purposes, but primarily it will assist those who are often forgotten but still affected by war: the families of our servicemen and women. The organization will host returned warriors and their families for a program that helps them re-connect both as a family unit and as members of our society. It will also provide a camp for children of veterans who have lost limbs that has counselors who have lost limbs themselves. WLF aims to humanize and celebrate their parents' sacrifice; rather than victimize and pity their injuries.

HELP THOSE WHO SERVE

WLP recognizes that returning from war is difficult and that support from family, friends, comrades and the society at large is vital for a successful transition. The organization will offer counseling, both professional and peer-to-peer, as well as a wealth of programs to allow the returning vets to ease their way out of battle mode. There will also be outdoor activities suitable for all including specific programs designed for wounded warriors.

How To Help

You can donate online or by check. Include "Luttrell Legacy Ranch" in your check's memo area.

Contact Information

First Western Trust Bank, DTC - Cherry Hills
c/o Warrior Legacy Foundation
5460 S. Quebec Street, Suite 200
Greenwood Village, CO 80111
info@warrriorlegacyfoundation.org
Website: www.warriorlegacyfoundation.org
Donations: www.warriorlegacyfoundation.org/donations

#92

Get Your Children Involved

Summary

You can engage you children in any number of child-friendly activities represented by the organizations in this book. Getting children involved teaches community service skills, world affairs, patriotism and activism.

Description

Most of us embrace the idea of teaching our children the value of community service and global awareness. You can accomplish that goal and more by introducing your children to some of the projects in *Help the Cause*.

How To Help

Explain to your children that they have the power to make a difference in someone's life. Cell Phones for Soldiers, an organization profiled in this book, was started by Robbie and Brittany Bergquist when they were just 12 and 13 years old.

There are any number of ways children can raise money for a cause. But the first step is choosing the right project. So many of the programs detailed in this book directly help the children and families of Afghanistan.

Your children can raise money for school supplies, or to help send Afghan girls to school. They can buy Afghan families livestock so the families can sell milk or chickens so the families can sell eggs. If your children knit, they can help keep Afghan children warm by sending blankets, sweaters, socks and hats through afghans for Afghans.

Another easy way to get involved is to have the children draw pictures or write letters to our troops. There are numerous organizations profiled in this book that will provide you with names and addresses or mail the letters for you.

You can also discuss what common items service members need, and hold a goods drive to collect items to make care packages. The children can write letters to local businesses and ask for goods donations as well.

GET INVOLVED

Spirit of America has many active projects, initiated by our troops, to help the people of Afghanistan. Your child could adopt a project and raise funds for that specific initiative. Spirit of America will keep your child posted on progress.

Some fun ideas for fundraising can range from the classic lemonade stand or bake sale to creating artwork for customized cards, a fundraising chain letter, selling labels and photo books. Half the fun is coming up with ideas.

Contact Information

afghans for Afghans: www.afghansforafghans.org
Spirit of America: www.spiritofamerica.net
A Million Thanks: www.amillionthanks.org

#93

Get Your Classroom Involved

Summary

You can get your children's classroom involved in projects that will benefit the people of Afghanistan and our troops.

Description

Whether you are a teacher, or just have children in school, you can help get kids involved in charitable causes. Not only do the children learn valuable lessons about helping others, they also learn that they have the power to make a difference. By supporting projects in this book, there is also an opportunity to teach history and geography lessons.

How To Help

Parents, contact your children's teachers and discuss ways that the classroom can get involved in helping a charitable organization. Teachers, find an age-appropriate project that you think your classroom will be most interested in and able to understand.

One you have picked your project, get the kids involved!

First, talk about the reasons why the group you are aiming to help needs assistance. This is a great time to involve lessons about history and geography. Create an open forum for the children to discuss how they feel about helping. Explain to the kids that they have the power to make a difference in someone's life.

You can have your classroom sponsor an Afghan child for the year. Charities like War Kids Relief provide lesson plans and educational material that allow American classrooms to learn about other cultures as they help an Afghan child attend school.

Another easy way to get involved is to have the children draw pictures or write letters to our troops. There are numerous organizations profiled in this book that will provide you with names and addresses or mail the letters for you.

GET INVOLVED

You can also discuss what common items service members need, and hold a goods drive to collect items to make care packages. The children can write letters to local businesses and ask for goods donations as well.

You may decide that your classroom would like to make the commitment to send letters and packages regularly throughout the year. Soldiers' Angels allows classrooms to adopt a Soldier, and often the Soldier will correspond with the kids. Use a map to help kids visualize where their Soldier is located. It's also a chance to learn more about the people and culture of another country.

Operation Gratitude, based in Los Angeles, California offers many volunteer opportunities that could be a good fit for your classroom, including assembling care packages and writing personal notes to servicemen and women.

There is no limit to the ways that a classroom can make a difference in the life of a service member or Afghan child.

If your public school does not have the supplies the children need to complete their project, contact DonorsChoose.org. The website allows teachers to post their requests online. When the funding goal is met, the school will receive the supplies.

Contact Information

Soldiers' Angels: www.soldiersangels.org
War Kids Relief: www.warkidsrelief.org
DonorsChoose.org: www.donorschoose.org
Operation Gratitude: www.opgratitude.com

#94

Get Your Company Involved

Summary

Your company can support your efforts to help an organization or project in *Help the Cause*.

Description

Many corporations have programs that benefit charities. You can use your company's charitable matching programs and service hours for the benefit of an organization in *Help the Cause*. You can ask your company to donate needed goods listed in the book.

How To Help

Contact your HR department and get all the details about your company's charitable efforts. One of the most common programs is matching donations. If you can show that you donated to charity, many companies will give the same amount. It is an easy way to double every gift you give.

Another program many companies have in place is time off for service. You may be allowed to take a few hours or a day off from work if you can prove that you are donating your time to a good cause.

The federal holiday honoring Dr. Martin Luther King, Jr. is a national day of service recognized as the King Day of Service. It is the perfect opportunity for your office to join together and get involved in supporting one of the 101 ways to help described in this book.

If your company does not have any programs in place, find out how you can change that. You might need to gather support from your co-workers, but businesses, no matter how large or small, benefit from these programs too.

Do some research, and present the appropriate executive with a list of reasons they need to become more involved in charitable efforts. Since they will likely be thinking about the bottom-line, here are a few tips to get you started.

GET INVOLVED

- Donations are tax deductible.
- Supporting a charity can garner great press: Yes, this is a selfish reason, but companies rely on profits to keep going. It never hurts to have a positive article written about you.
- Additional business: A better public image can equate to more business.
- Improves employee morale: Employees appreciate that the company they work for cares about helping others. Company-sponsored events also give employees the chance to spend time together outside of the office.

#95

Host a Book Discussion

Summary

You can open a dialog about ways to help the troops and communities in Afghanistan by hosting a book discussion about *Help the Cause*.

Description

Creating a book discussion group is a great way to encourage people to read this book, and then explore how they would like to help Afghan communities and support our troops.

How To Help

Contact your family and friends and tell them you are going to host a book discussion. Encourage them to bring their friends to the event. You can also put up notices on community bulletin boards, in the library, or even make an announcement in your local paper. Just be sure to let everyone know where they can purchase the book, when and where the event will be held, and what you'd like them to bring.

Whether the book event is a simple afternoon discussion over lemonade or a dinner party with wine and dessert, the important fact is that you are raising awareness.

Discuss the individual ways that each person has been motivated to make a difference. It can be very interesting to learn which projects each person found most compelling.

This book also provides many ways for groups to take on a project together. Sometimes people are hesitant to take action on their own, but will get involved with a little encouragement from their friends.

You can also talk about the local ways your group can help the cause. Each person has unique skills they can offer. A lawyer could offer some free advice to a veteran, a hairstylist could offer a free make-over to a returning service

GET INVOLVED

member, and an electrician could help modify an injured veteran's home. What could your group do if you all joined together?

If you enjoy your book discussion, you can always turn it into a reoccurring book club. Figure out what topic you'd like to explore. Perhaps you'd like to read more about the struggles of the people of Afghanistan. Maybe you'd like to learn about other countries whose women are fighting for improved rights. Or perhaps you would like to find other books about the stories of our service members. A quick trip to your library or search on Amazon.com will yield many possibilities.

#96

Raise Funds

Summary

You can raise funds to support your favorite projects from *Help the Cause*.

Description

There are a variety of ways that you can raise funds to support your favorite causes. By getting the word out about your fundraiser, you also help bring awareness to the organization you are supporting.

How To Help

The ways in which you can raise money for your favorite cause are endless. Brainstorm with friends and search for ideas online to find a fundraising idea that you like the best. Just remember to explain that all money raised will be going to a good cause. It helps to provide information about the organization you're supporting at the event. Here are some ideas to get you started:

Yard Sale: This can also be a great way to do a little spring cleaning. If you have boxes collecting dust in your basement or attic, pull them out and see what you can live without. If you haven't used an item in the last year, ask yourself if you really need it. This is also a fun way to get kids involved. Explain the importance of helping others, and see if they have any toys or books that they no longer use. Ask your neighbors if they would be interested in joining you. Be sure to get the word out about your sale. Think about placing an ad in the newspaper, call the local radio station and ask them to make an announcement, and put out posters and balloons the day of the sale.

Concert/Performing Arts Show: Contact the talented people in your community and see if they are interested in putting together a concert, talent contest, play, or dance recital. Ask a local school if they would donate the use of their auditorium for the event. Ask the art department if they would make posters to help advertise. Charge admission and let the community know that all proceeds

GET INVOLVED

go to your favorite charity.

Bake Sale: Put your culinary skills to good use. Bake items that are easy to eat and package. Ask your friends to help you, and set up a table at sporting events and community fairs. It would also be a great addition to a charity concert.

Raffle: Contact the local businesses in your area and see what items or services they would be willing to donate. Raffle off tickets, or create a silent auction, for the donated items.

Golf or Poker Tournament: Find a hobby that you enjoy, perhaps golfing or poker, and organize a game for charity. Find a venue that will donate the use of their space, and consider gathering donated items for prizes to increase participation.

Collection Jar: If you don't have time to organize a large event, you can start small and encourage everyday giving. Put a collection jar on your desk at work, and ask your co-workers to drop in their spare change each day. Try only using paper money, and always break a new dollar. By not using exact change, your pennies will add up faster. See of your colleagues will do the same. If you work in a service job, get permission to place a collection jar by the register. Be sure to put the name and a short description of the charity on the jar.

#97

Shop with Charities in Mind

Summary

You can give charitable donations when you buy someone a gift.

Description

Shopping can be a good way to donate to charity. Many of the organizations featured in the book have special programs where you can make donations. From gift catalogs to giving cards, there are a variety of alternatives to straight cash donations.

How To Help

Shop Online

Did you know that you can help the organizations in this book just by shopping? It's that easy. GoodShop is an online shopping mall of world-class merchants dedicated to helping fund worthy causes across the country. You simply type in the name of the organization you would like to support, and then continue on to buy the items you were looking for. Each purchase made via the GoodShop mall results in a donation – averaging approximately 3% of the sale, but going up to 20% or more.

If you're not ready to make a purchase, do your research through GoodSearch. The search engine, powered by Yahoo!, works like any other search engine except that half of the advertising revenue it makes goes to charity. Just like GoodShop, you can choose the charity you would like to receive your donation.

Redeem Credit Card Points

Many credit card companies have special cards associated with charities and foundations. Charity credit cards usually work like any other rewards cards, except that the rewards don't go to you, but to the charity or foundation with which the card is associated. Even standard credit cards with reward points may have a charitable gifting option. Instead of redeeming your points for a discount

GET INVOLVED

coupon or cash back, consider giving to a charity. Each credit card is different, so check with your provider to see what options are available.

Buy a Giving Card

Giving cards make great gifts and help support great causes. They allow you to give a charitable contribution to a project or organization that the recipient chooses. You pick the amount you wish to give, and the recipient decides where to donate it. And like regular charitable contributions, giving cards are usually tax-deductable.

Charity Choice is a website that allows you to buy giving cards that are redeemable for more than 100 different charities. Mercy Corp, CARE, Save the Children, Disabled American Veterans (DAV), Operation Homefront, Special Operations Warrior Foundation and USO are just some of the organizations on the site that we have profiled in this book.

Contact Information

GoodShop: www.goodsearch.com/goodshop.aspx
GoodSearch: www.goodsearch.com
Charity Choice: www.charitygiftcertificates.org

#98

Talk to a Veteran About Their Story

Summary

You can show a veteran that you are interested in his/her personal story by asking them to sit down and talk. You can also learn a great deal about the people living in the war-torn countries.

Description

Some veterans enjoy talking about their experience serving their country. Their experiences are part of our nation's history and can provide great insight into the ideals and trials and tribulations of our servicemen and women. Keep in mind that not every service member is interested in sharing their story.

How To Help

The first thing to do when talking to a veteran is to thank them for their service. Then, ask if they are comfortable talking about their experiences. If the veteran would rather not talk to you, do not take it personally. If he or she does agree to talk with you, respect their decision to not answer certain questions.

It is best to begin the conversation with a few general questions and let the conversation progress from there. A good way to start is to ask some background questions, such as what branch of the service they were in, what war they served in, and how old they were when they enlisted.

It is important to remember that every veteran is different, and there is no rule book that can walk you through the process. But if you do find someone willing to talk with you, it can be an enriching experience.

If you know someone who would like to share his/her experience, you can also ask if they would like to submit their story to the Library of Congress' Veterans History Project. The project aims to collect personal stories from veterans so

GET INVOLVED

future generations can hear first-hand accounts of war and better understand the courage and sacrifice of our service members. Veterans may submit their own stories, or may do so through an interviewer like you.

After registering, you can download and print the Veterans History Project Field Kit. You will also find instructions on how to prepare for and conduct an interview. Since the projected began, more than 65,000 individual personal accounts have been recorded.

Contact Information

Library of Congress Veterans History Project: www.loc.gov/vets

#99

Write a Letter to the Editor

Summary

You can express your thanks to our service members or encourage your community to help the cause by writing to your local newspaper.

Description

If you are motivated and passionate about the work that our service members are doing or want to call attention to the need to help the Afghan people, you can express your opinion in your local paper. Writing a letter to the editor or submitting an Op-Ed (opinion piece or editorial) can get your voice heard.

How To Help

Write to your local paper and express your opinion, or encourage your community to take action. While there is no guarantee that your letter will appear in the paper, there are several steps you can take to increase your chances.

You can find contact information and submission guidelines in your newspaper, and often on the newspaper's website.

1. Find a topic you feel strongly about, and keep the letter focused on that one idea.

2. Gather your thoughts on paper and do your research. Your letter will have more credibility if you can back up your thoughts with a few facts.

3. Include your major points in the first few paragraphs as letters may be edited to fit available space.

4. Let your passion and emotion come through in your letter, but do not begin to rant. Putting other people down and calling names will only distance your readers.

5. Re-read your finished letter several times to check for clarity and grammatical errors. When you are sure there are no mistakes, read it one more time.

GET INVOLVED

6. Include your name, address, and phone number. The editor will likely want to verify that you wrote the letter before it is published.

#100

Give *Help the Cause* as a Gift

Summary

You can give *Help the Cause* as a gift to family, friends, co-workers and your local library.

Description

When you have been inspired, it is easy to get others to share your enthusiasm. We hope that after reading this book, you want to share that excitement with your family, friends, and even your community. Giving copies of *Help the Cause* as gifts is a great way to do this.

Just by purchasing the book, you are making a financial contribution that will help to implement change. 100% of the proceeds from sale of the book go directly to projects and needs in Afghanistan and to support our troops.

Many of the important people in your life would probably like to help the people of Afghanistan or our troops who serve there, but either don't know how or feel their support won't make a real difference. You may have even felt that way before reading this book. By giving a copy of *Help the Cause*, you will let them know they can make a direct and meaningful impact.

Each story you have read is about the hopes and struggles of the Afghan people; the initiative and courage of organizations working to help; and the extraordinary work and sacrifice of American troops. Every small step you take to help the cause supports these efforts.

Consider buying books for your community or school library, for the waiting room in your doctor's office, or for the lobby of your workplace.

GET INVOLVED

How to Help

You can purchase additional copies of *Help the Cause* online at www.helpthecause.com. If you're interested in buying *Help the Cause* in quantity, visit the web site for information on discount rates.

Contact Information

Help the Cause
www.helpthecause.com

#101

Tell Your Story at helpthecause.com

Summary

Share your experience helping the cause and let others learn from, and be inspired by, what you've done.

Description

We hope you'll be part of a larger discussion about how people can help the cause. We want to hear from you because your experiences can inspire others to take action!

How To Help

Tell us about your experience when you:

- thank a veteran for their service
- ask your company to donate goods for one of the projects in *Help the Cause*
- give copies of Help the Cause as gifts to your friends
- send a letter to your newspaper's editor
- volunteer for an organization related to helping the cause
- host a book salon to discuss Help the Cause
- rally your child's classroom or school to support one of the ways to help
- call into a radio show
- buy a beer or a burger for one of our troops
- inspire your family or community to help

Tell us about your favorite way to help. What stories compelled you to do something?

If you know of a great organization or initiative that we haven't included in the book, let us know that too.

GET INVOLVED

How to Help

Go to www.helpthecause.com and click on "Tell Your Story."

Contact Information

Help the Cause
www.helpthecause.com

SPIRIT OF AMERICA

Spirit of America, the publisher of *Help the Cause,* is a 501c3 nonprofit charity founded in 2003. Spirit of America's mission is to help Americans serving abroad assist people in need.

Spirit of America receives and fulfills requests from Americans serving in Afghanistan, Iraq and Africa for goods that will help local people. At the request of American troops, Spirit of America has provided a broad range of humanitarian assistance - sewing machines, irrigation equipment, farm tools, shoes and sandals, hospital equipment, medical supplies, school supplies, clothing, blankets and more – all for the benefit of local citizens.

Often referred to as helping "win hearts and minds," Spirit of America's support saves lives and improves relations between our troops and the local people where they serve. In addition to its humanitarian benefit, this support plays an important role in the counterinsurgency (COIN) strategy of our troops in Afghanistan.

Spirit of America allows donors to earmark their donations for specific projects and needs. Donors thus have the assurance that 100% of their contribution is used for the direct expenses of the designated purpose. Contributions to Spirit of America projects in Afghanistan will only be used to purchase and ship the goods requested by American servicemen and women for the benefit of the Afghan people.

Spirit of America
www.spiritofamerica.net
staff@spiritofamerica.net

ACKNOWLEDGEMENTS

This book began as an extension of my work at Spirit of America where we provide specific, targeted ways for people to support our troops and help the people of Afghanistan, Iraq and Africa. Spirit of America's small, dedicated staff of Peggy Findley, Michele Redmond and Natasha Norman identified many of the ways to help that are featured in *Help the Cause*. Their work and commitment make a difference every day.

Spirit of America has four retired Marines helping as volunteers: Col. David Couvillon (Couv), LtCol. Al Burghard, Capt. Chris Lohmann and Sgt. Christopher Ahn. Couv and Al deserve special recognition; they made our first two requests when they were serving in Iraq in 2003 and proved the Spirit of America concept would work.

Without Wendi Tush and Lindsey Gardner we never would have made our impossibly short book production deadlines. Their enthusiasm and belief in the value of *Help the Cause* propelled us to completion. Patricia Bacall worked quickly, cheerfully, and with great skill on the design and production of *Help the Cause*. Thanks to Ellen Steifler for putting us together. Pam Hicks, my sister, and Jim Bongard, my brother-in-law, dropped everything on a moment's notice to assist with research. Hugh Griffin and the team at Stuart F. Cooper printers provided outstanding service and the shortest-possible turnaround. Meredith Canniff, Cassell Kroll and Ellen Reid contributed to the book as well.

Sergeant First Class Jay Smith and U.S. Army Special Forces provided the inspiration for Spirit of America with their work helping the people of Orgun-e, Afghanistan in 2002.

Through Spirit of America I have had the privilege of working with and supporting many of America's Soldiers, Sailors, Airmen and Marines. Their service, sacrifice and abilities are awe-inspiring. What we, as a country, ask of them is impossible. And yet they deliver every day.

I was extraordinarily lucky to meet Marine General Jim Mattis and Lt. General Joe Dunford in Spirit of America's early days. They are examples of leadership, commitment and service that I strive to emulate. Both men give great cause for pride in our country.

Dan Henninger of *The Wall Street Journal* has been an invaluable supporter of Spirit of America. He saw the potential impact of our work early on and helped bring it to the attention of the American people.

Ambassador Mark Palmer, partner and Advisor to Spirit of America, has a cheerful optimism and principled commitment to freedom and democracy that set the standard for diplomats around the world.

Don Karl, serving on the Spirit of America Board, has provided great assistance and encouragement to the Spirit of America team. Mark Thompson's excellent work on leadership has been of great service.

The generous support and outstanding service of FedEx has made it possible for Spirit of America to quickly respond to requests from American troops in Iraq and Afghanistan.

Donovan Janus and Rhesa Rozendaal built Spirit of America's web site and despite being fully engaged in a new business still find time to help. Barton Listick has been of tremendous assistance on all aspects of Spirit of America. Doug Franco and Orchard International contributed greatly to Spirit of America's work in Iraq and Afghanistan.

Captain John and Laurie McCaull, my father- and mother-in-law, immediately grasped the concept for Spirit of America in early 2003. Laurie was our first evangelist. She got the ear of Ambassador Diana Lady Dougan, who took Spirit of America under her wing so we could start up quickly and easily as a project of the Cyber Century Forum.

My wife Kristy is an amazing artist and great mother. She is also my sweetheart, so regardless of what is happening in the world, I always know I have that going for me. Our sons Sam and Muki are the two finest young men a father could ever hope to have.

Without my brother, Frank Hake, Spirit of America would not have gotten off the ground. If only his football picking skills were equal to his great business acumen.

I learned a remarkable amount from my partners Bruce Eames and Frank Crivello. At Access Media we applied the collective approach evidenced in *Help the Cause*, bringing together different organizations behind a common goal. Mitch Ratcliffe and Seth Rosenblatt brought together Access Media and SOFTBANK for which I'll always be thankful.

I would be remiss not to acknowledge my fellow USA Brothers: Michael Bigham, John Moragne, David Chute, Ralph Tolson, Jim Coulter and Chip Debelius. We didn't invent the expression "is this a great country or what?" but we have tried our best to honor it.

I had the great benefit of growing up with the love and support of my parents, Babs and Jim Hake. I miss them both. My mother didn't live to see Spirit of America get started but I know she's looking down with pride, hopefully while enjoying a hot dog and potato chips. My father served in WWII as part of the Navy's 1006th Special SeaBee Detachment. His sense of humor, love of life and can-do, anything-is-possible attitude will always serve as my foundation.

INDEX